India and Turkmenistan

India and Turkmenistan

Cooperation for Peace and Development in the Silk Road Region

Edited by

Manu Mittal
Mona Agnihotri

SHIPRA

Rs. 800; US$ 40

ISBN: 978-81-7541-882-0

First Published in India in 2017

India and Turkmenistan: Cooperation for Peace and Development in the Silk Road Region

Published by:
SHIPRA PUBLICATIONS
LG 18-19, Pankaj Central Market
I.P. Ext., Patparganj, Delhi 110092, India
Tel.: +91 11 2223 5152/6152
E-mail: info@shiprapublication.com
www.shiprapublication.com

Dedicated
to all
who have journeyed
through time on the Silk Road

Foreword

It is my great pleasure to mention that this book of articles "*India and Turkmenistan: Cooperation for Peace and Development in the Silk Road Region*" is about the matters of common concern—universal peace and stability, economic and social prosperity, common energy security, unconstrained access to markets and effective utilization of available transport and transit corridors. Besides, I wish that the reader would discover the intensity of Turkmenistan-Hindistan's (as we call her) deeply rooted and centuries old historical, cultural and economic bilateral exchange and mutual cooperation and how our destinies were intertwined in the past and continue their journeys today.

I would like to take the opportunity to express my gratitude to the Silk Road Studies Programme of Jawaharlal Nehru University, New Delhi for providing all assistance in editing and publishing this book.

Above all, my deep appreciation goes to the Honourable President of Turkmenistan Gurbanguly Berdimuhamedov for consistently pursuing Permanent Neutrality and Open Door foreign policy and reformist domestic socio-economic policies aimed at enhancement of quality of life of every national of Turkmenistan, maintaining his political and economic sovereignty and independence!

I am sure that the articles published in this book, which are by eminent experts from both Turkmenistan and India will contribute significantly to our understanding of common linkages across different subjects.

I also would like to thank the Ambassador Amangeldi Rahmanov, who was the first Turkmen Ambassador to hoist our flag at the UN Headquarters in New York in 1992 and who played a crucial role in my life as well at that time and continues to mentor me since then. I thank him for his article in this book. I am sure that he has a lot to share with us.

I would also like to highlight that Turkmens were deeply connected with India, created numerous Sultanates, especially in the North and South of the country. Existence of Great Silk Route, and Merv as the major transit point between East and West and North and South, as well as cultural exchanges between Ancient Indian Civilizations and those found in Turkmenistan, like Margush or Margiana stood the tests of time gone by and have survived till today.

It is also worth mentioning that in the year 2015 Merv has been declared as a Cultural Capital of the Turkic World. Today, Turkmenistan and India actively promote cultural exchange and Days of Culture and film screenings and other activities take place annually to promote these strong ties.

I am sure that many of you must be aware that we have declared the year 2015 as a "Year Neutrality and Peace" in commemoration of the 20th Anniversary of the status of Permanent Neutrality, which is self-imposed and is the only one that is unanimously recognized at the United Nations General Assembly on December 12, 1995, via its Resolution "Permanent Neutrality of Turkmenistan". Since then Neutrality became a part of our Constitution. This was a historic event. The undeniable fact is that Turkmenistan's foreign policy has universal international support. Turkmenistan is now one of the recognized peacekeeping centers not only in Central Asia but also in the world. The establishment of the UN Regional Centre for Preventive Diplomacy for Central Asia in 2007 at Ashgabat expanded its role in this field globally as well.

Having its foundation on the neutral status, Turkmenistan is consistently widening its international, political, trade and economic relations. Based on the "Concept of the Foreign Policy of Turkmenistan for the Years 2013-2017", Asia-Pacific Region has its due recognition. So far we have established diplomatic relations with 134 counties and trade with more than 103.

As pointed out by the President of Turkmenistan at a meeting of the Council of Elders last fall, neutral Turkmenistan enjoys full support from the international community in matters related to promotion of global peace, security and sustainable development.

Turkmenistan offers to convene Forum on Security and Peace in the Central Asian Region under the auspices of the United Nations and is considering the establishment of the United Nations Interregional Center on Disarmament in Asia.

In areas of energy security and transport-transit corridors, Turkmenistan stands ready to provide ample energy to India to quench its thirst for energy and the thirst of any other country in between. Turkmenistan-Afghanistan-Pakistan-India (TAPI) gas pipeline must be looked at as an attempt not only to supply vital energy to the booming region but also as our aspiration to diversify our markets and use those revenues for diversifying national economy by doing away from supplying raw material to value addition.

Transportation which remains at the center stage of global economy and politics with the international proposals of my country, which in fact was recognized by the community of nations in December 2014 at the 69th UNGA Session via the special Resolution on transport and transit corridors to serve the aims of sustainable development. It is based on the idea that Turkmenistan becomes a transport hub of regional and interregional importance. For example, multimodal transportation corridors running through my country easily connect Afghanistan with Baltic Sea, Uzbekistan with Black Sea, Kazakhstan with high seas of Indian Ocean - rest I just leave to your imagination.

Neutral Turkmenistan also attaches great importance to international cooperation in humanitarian field, specifically in matters related to the health of a mother and a child, protection of the rights of the disabled, refugees and displaced people. In the years 2011-2014 Turkmenistan granted citizenship to about five thousand people.

Turkmenistan also pays close attention to the issues related to ecology and environmental protection. It supports implementation of joint activities to improve the environmental situation in Central Asia and the Caspian region and the level and quality of life. During the 69th UN General Assembly Session Turkmenistan proposed development of effective mechanisms for enhanced cooperation on environmental issues and suggested creation of an Inter-Regional Center to address issues related to climate change.

In the end, I would like to emphasize the importance of being neutral for Turkmenistan and our ability to share the benefits of such policy for common prosperity. This book should be a wonderful opportunity to provide a platform for a debate on Neutrality and hope that our cooperation results in better understanding of the needs of others and opportunities that, I am sure, we all possess.

Parakhat H. Durdyev
Ambassador of Turkmenistan to India

Preface

I am delighted to say that this book is being published at a time when the world finds itself at the cross roads of history. Arab Spring in the Middle East has metamorphosed into an Arabic Winter. A chill has set in. No clear direction is visible. Iraq and Syria are up in flames. Enormous uncertainty surrounds developments in Afghanistan with gradual and progressive withdrawal of US, NATO and ISAF (International Security Assistance Force) forces. Turkmenistan stands in the middle of these two regions as a beacon, and if I may borrow a phrase from the terrain and ecology of Middle East and Central Asia, is an oasis of peace. In addition, its economy has been growing at an enviable and impressive pace of 10-12% every year over the last few years. This is particularly commendable as many countries in the region as also in the industrialized and developed world are trying to come to terms with the international economic and financial crisis that struck the world in 2007-2008 and the EU sovereign debt crisis that started in 2009-2010. The end of neither of these crises is in sight.

With its vast gas reserves, Turkmenistan also provides an answer to ensure energy security to energy deficient countries like India whose demands are growing at a rapid pace because of the rapid expansion of their economies.

Turkmenistan is a land locked State and has over the last eight years since it joined the North-South International Transport Corridor worked to construct railways to create a seamless network from Kazakhstan to Iran extending right up to the Arabian Sea.

India is a natural and perfect ally and partner to Turkmenistan. India's economy has been growing at an impressive pace since the beginning of this century. There might have been a hiatus in our growth trajectory for a few years after 2010 because of the perceived policy drift and a large number of corruption scandals and scams, but today with the principal ruling party having a comfortable majority in the Lok Sabha – the lower house of parliament – and looking at the performance of our stock market and buoyant market sentiment, we are firmly on the trajectory of high economic growth. Prime Minister Modi's foreign policy over the past nine months has amply demonstrated that India is pro-actively reaching out not only to its neighbours in SAARC, but also to other major players like USA, Russia, Japan, China, Australia and Europe to promote peace, security, stability and prosperity, not only in our country, but also in the world.

In this context, partnership and collaboration between India and Turkmenistan assume special significance and importance. India's Connect Central Asia Policy has been there since 2012. Now is the time to assess how much we have achieved as a result of this policy. The general feeling is that while the Policy identifies several eminently desirable elements, implementation could be made more rigorous, energetic and dynamic.

Relations between India and Turkmenistan are ancient, historical and civilizational, spanning over several centuries and millennia. What is required is to translate and transform these friendly and deep rooted relations into current day realities. We need to take full advantage of all the opportunities available and potential to take them to thus far uncharted heights. Implementation of the Turkmenistan – Afghanistan – Pakistan – India (TAPI) gas pipeline on which discussions have been going on for the last several years is of crucial significance.

It is understood that a visit from India to Turkmenistan at the highest political level might be taking place in the coming months.

This will provide a strong fillip to bilateral ties. The only travel by an Indian Prime Minister over the last 25 years since Turkmenistan became a sovereign, independent country was by the then Prime Minister Narasimha Rao in 1995. It is expected that during the forthcoming visit, in addition to important issues like TAPI, subjects of connectivity with Central Asia and Russia through Iran and the Integrated North South Transport Corridors (INSTC); urgent need to promote peace, security, stability in Afghanistan; fight against terrorism and radicalization, and economic and trade cooperation will be discussed. Deliberations at the highest level will help both the countries to skillfully navigate the shifting sands and changing contours of regional politics and security dynamics.

I think that it is important to recognize that Positive and Permanent Neutrality being pursued by Turkmenistan does not imply total non-affiliation with international issues. On December 12, 1995, the UN General Assembly for the first time in its history adopted the Special Resolution on "the Permanent Neutrality of Turkmenistan" as recognition of the peaceful foreign policy of the country and its significant contribution to the peaceful development of international relations, global security and progress.

Ashok Sajjanhar
President, Institute of Global Studies,
Former Ambassador of India to
Kazakhstan, Sweden and Latvia,
Former Secretary/Principal Executive Officer,
National Foundation for Communal Harmony,
Government of India

Acknowledgements

On behalf of the Silk Road Studies Programme, Jawaharlal Nehru University (SRSP, JNU), I thank all who have joined this journey in revisiting the important historical as well as contemporary role played by India and Turkmenistan in the Silk Road Regions. The civilizations of these two nations contributed in connecting as well as enriching the flow of trade, precious merchandise, culture, religion, language, thought, and people who travelled along the fabled network of routes of the Silk Road, traversing some of the toughest terrains over desolate deserts and high mountain corridors.

While on one hand, the book recalls the historic geopolitical and cultural links between India and Turkmenistan, the contributors have delved deep into history, capturing current realities to visualise and project possibilities for a contemporary Silk Road built on international cooperation for lasting development, peace and prosperity in this *Common Culture Region.* I take this opportunity to thank all who have contributed to this book or have been associated with it in different capacities.

I am grateful to the Jawaharlal Nehru University and the Embassy of Turkmenistan in India for creating a forum at the SRSP, JNU for discussions from where this book evolved. I also acknowledge with gratitude the constant support and encouragement of H.E. Parakhat Durdyev, the Ambassador of Turkmenistan in India and the then Vice Chancellor of the Jawaharlal Nehru University Prof. S.K. Sopory.

I thank Jawaharlal Nehru University for providing a publication grant that has made this book possible. The articles in this book reflect the views of the authors and not of JNU or the editors.

Manu Mittal
Convenor
Silk Road Studies Programme
Jawaharlal Nehru University
New Delhi.

Contents

Transport Corridor and Regional Cooperation

Culture, History and Philosophy

Region

Introduction

It is indeed my privilege to thank the experts and authors, who, through their valuable contributions, made this book a success, and made our journey to revisit ties between India and Turkmenistan a memorable one. This book is also about a time of celebration - the year 2015 marked two decades of recognition by the UN of the Permanent Neutrality of Turkmenistan, and also two decades of Turkmenistan's membership to the Non-Aligned Movement while we approach nearly twenty years of our mutual diplomatic relations; relations that have a great depth of cultural and historical links.

Central Asia and more specifically Turkmenistan, through which the routes of the Silk Road traversed, has always been alive in the Indian subconscious, and the Silk Road, a corridor of history and civilization, beckons us to a future born from our shared heritage. The fabled Silk Road is a unique example from history of inter-continental collaboration, and the regions of the Silk Road form an extended neighbourhood bound by common historic and cultural destinies. The network of roads brought together traders and served as a channel for meeting of civilizations, and the cross migration of people and ideas left an indelible impact on our lives today. With people moved languages and cuisine, ways of life and arts, belief and religion, and thus evolved the 'road of the dialogue'.

Time has seen the boundaries of empires change across the Indo-Central Asian region—to the current times, where as Sovereign Nations the countries of the region have exciting prospects of co-operation and further cementing their deep-rooted bonds.

Given this background, the study of the Silk Road and related subjects is the focus of the Silk Road Studies Programme (SRSP) at JNU. The SRSP is a multi-disciplinary initiative that seeks to address the pressing need for an intensive yet broad based approach towards political, economic, and cultural connections that weave together the 'Common Culture Regions' of the Silk Road.

India and Turkmenistan

The archaeological findings from Altyn Depe reveal connections from a pre-Kushan period; Bairam Khan, mentor of the great Emperor Akbar, was from Turkmenistan and his son—Rahim Khan-i-Khana, was one of the 'Navrattanas'—or wise men—in the court of Emperor Akbar whose verses continue to be revered in India even today. The city of Hyderabad was founded by Turkmen Sultan Mohammad Quli. Even today, the Turkman Gate in Delhi reminds us of the great historical ties between our countries. When we read the poetry of great thinkers, such as Magtymguly Pyragy of Turkmenistan and Kabir, Surdas and poets of Bhaktikal in India, we find much similarity in their thoughts and expressions. 'Hindustan' finds fond and prominent mention in poems by Magtymguly Pyragy—great Turkmen poet - over three centuries ago.

As we march together towards the future, our countries, with the new-age realities, strategic locations and abundance of natural resources face similar challenges underlining the need to explore our commonalities and revitalize our connections. ...And thus, the 'Silk Road' that knit this region into one, again finds itself in focus.

Neutrality and Peace

India has attached great importance to its relations with Turkmenistan, and was amongst the first countries to recognize its independence. There is a common global vision that the two countries share—India is a supporter of Turkmenistan's policy of positive neutrality, and the doctrine compliments India's outlook towards regional and global security, cooperation and development.

President Gurbanguly Berdimuhamedov regards the Non-Aligned Movement as crucial in the development of Turkmenistan's positive neutrality—thus, our foreign policies also have a common root of inspiration. India, through its 'Connect Central Asia Policy' desires to engage stakeholders for development in the Indo-Central Asian region. Turkmenistan has always been the 'Gateway to Central Asia'.

As we marked 2015 as the Year of Neutrality and Peace, I conclude with the thought that the silk-strings that bind the people of the region along the Silk Road together are those of relationships and common destinies. We must work together to weave a new tapestry of peace, progress and harmony. For, this has bearing on all the regions of the Silk Road.

Manu Mittal

Politics, Neutrality and Peace

Silk Road Region

Turkmenistan and India

Manu Mittal

Turkmenistan, India and whole of Central Asia - Regions of the fabled Silk Road have formed an extended neighbourhood bound by common historic and cultural destinies.

In today's dynamic global scenario, these regions of Central Asia and the Caucasus, with their strategic location, rich natural resources and resurgent economies are once again in focus. There is an urgent need of greater cultural and people to people interaction, trade and economic treaties, political and strategic alliances, and enhanced cooperation amongst the Silk Road countries and neighbouring regions.

As work is going on to re-vitalize and renew the unique international and intercontinental cooperation that the Silk Road historically symbolizes, it is imperative to remember that besides the trade and commerce that took place, the most important exchange to move along the Silk Road, - far subtler yet stronger than the Silk it carried —was that of ideas and culture... And to this exchange of thought, religion and culture, India's interaction and contribution have been immense.

Historical Overview

High mountain corridors and the trade routes that form the Silk Road have connected the regions across the Himalayas and the Pamirs since antiquity. Similarities have been found between the Neolithic cultures of Kangra Valley in India and Gissan (Hissar) of Central Asia. Around 3500 BC a 'Common Painted Pottery Civilization' is said to have existed right across Asia from Egypt – Mesopotamia - Indus Valley - to China. Later, around 2000 - 1500 BC, the Aryans are believed to have come from Central Asia and settled in India and Iran with close trade and cultural relations between these regions. The ancient Indian hymns of the Vedas, and the great Indian epics the Ramayana and Mahabharata (c. 1700-1500 B.C.), the teachings in the *Upanishadas*[1] as well as later day Sanskrit literature have innumerable references to places, persons, kingdoms, ethnic groups and practices of Central Asian Region. Influence of Indian culture was reflected in geographical names, folklore, ethical code and everyday life in Central Asia. There was cross migration of communities across the region.

There seems to have been contact between the Indus valley and Central Asia predating the arrival of the Aryans in India. Excavations in centres of Harappan civilization in northwest region of India – Pakistan, reveal evidence of inter tribal exchange of goods. It appears that Harappans acquired gems from Central Asia, and Harappan handicrafts, metal goods, beads made of faience (porcelain), pottery, ivory etc. have been found in sites in Central Asia where even the local items appear to have had an Indian influence.

References have been found in the *Rigveda*[2] (c 2000 B.C.) of the burial rituals and similar items used by Vedic tribes in these rituals

1. Upanishadas are speculative prose treatises in Sanskrit language which were composed between the 8th and 6th centuries B.C. www.dictionary.com/browse/upanishad, 4 May 2016
2. Rigveda is one of the Vedas (they are the entire body of Hindu sacred writings. There are four Vedas – the Rigveda, the Samaveda, the Atharvaveda and the Yajurveda) www.dictionay.com/browse/veda, 4 May 2016

have been found in excavations in northwest Indian and Central Asian sites. Discovery of iron-plated armours of 3rd–2nd c B.C. from Takhshila (now in Pakistan) indicate the presence of nomadic conquerors from the steppes of Eurasia in this region. The discovery of proto-Indian seal from Altyn-dep indicates that some people of Central Asia were able to read the 'Dravid' language of the Dravidians who lived in India before the Aryans. Cornelian beads discovered from Central Asian sites indicate that these beads were imported from India and Iran (Abuseitova, MK, 2004).

Ancient Indian epics and the *Puranas*[1] referring to Asia as Jambudvipa describe the Pamirs as Mount Meru and the adjoining areas; and how a mythological great churning of the seas was carried out by the Devas (gods), who held their conference on Mt. Meru. The great Indian epics Mahabharata and Ramayana both describe the Central Asian region at length.

Throughout history, the Yavanas (Greeks), the Sakas (Scythians, Slavs), the Hunas (Huns), Kushans (descendents of the Mongols), the Mongols and the Turks came to India from or through Central Asia. Similarly, ethnic communities migrated from India to the Central Asian regions. The descendents of the Shakas are a part of India as the Shakdveepi Brahmins, Chouhans, Banofer, Rajput – Gujjars and Jats. Another view holds that probably Shakas were of Indian origin and migrated to Central Asia (Kumar, B.B., 2004). These historical movements left an indelible impact on the Indian mind and culture as well as on that of Central Asia. Indians still officially use the Saka calendar. Linguistic similarities and the use of Indian dialects in Central Asia have been studied and documented.

That there was a two way movement of ethnic groups is being established through historical, linguistic, anthropological as well as the more recent genetic studies. While historians have traditionally believed that there was a male mediated genetic influx from Central Asia that set up the upper castes in the Indian Caste System, in a

1. Puranas are any of 18 colleections of Hindu legends and religious instructions www.dictionary.com/browse/puraana, 4 May 2016

ground breaking paper published in January, 2009, Professor. Bamezai and his team at the Centre of Applied Human Genetics at Jawaharlal Nehru University (JNU), New Delhi have demonstrated genetic linkages to confront this view and that Indian tribal genes may be more prevalent in Indian Brahmins, as also this supports the view that many of these ethnic groups may in fact have migrated from India to Eurasia.

It was the legendary Silk Road routes that facilitated these linkages and the spread of Buddhism to Central Asia and China, especially during Ashoka's (268-226 BC) and the Kushan (1 - 3 A.D.) Empires; and in the spread of Hindu thought and religious practices to Sogdiana (5 –9 A.D.). The Middle-Ages saw invaders like Mahmud Ghazni from Central Asia, Chengiz Khan from Mongolia; and later Temurlane from Uzbekistan who came to India, plundered and went back. However, others came and stayed such as Quli Qutub Shah from Turkoman who established the Sultanate at Hyderabad in the Deccan in South India, and later Babar from the Firghana Valley who established the Mughal Empire in India. Islam and the Central Asian thought, culture and cuisine came and blended with the local in India. Languages interacted and enriched each other and a new camp language - 'Urdu' was born that saw a large body of literature and fresh literary traditions grow.

The India-Central Asian interaction received a setback during British India and picked up only after the Indian Independence to flourish during the 60s to 80s of the Soviet times. However, after the collapse of the USSR the Central Asian – Indian relations are finding new meanings, dimensions and strengths in today's fast changing world scenario. The old Silk Road routes need revisiting. It is not just in Indian, but in regional and global interests to re-kindle these ancient socio-economic-cultural ties between India and Central Asia.

From the Indian perspective the interaction on the Silk Road was not limited to the trade of silks, gold, silver, diamonds and gems, jade, ceramics, glassware, yarn, cloth, furs, horses, livestock, incense, spices, fruit, exotic birds, and other valuables and precious material. The most important was the movement of idea and culture, of religion and tolerance, of languages and arts, of artists and artisans, of people, who came to India – and stayed…

The Turkmen poet Magtymguly Pyragy wrote extensively about India and its beauty; he also visited India.

Linguistic and Literary Linkages

There are a large number of references to the continuous Central Asian – Indian links in Sanskrit literature. More than a thousand words of Russian and Central Asian languages similar to words in Sanskrit, with most having the same root in Sanskrit, have been listed by the Indian scholar Rahul Sanskritayan. The author's own work has further identified another few hundred words common to or having common roots in Indian and Central Asian languages. Some studies have pointed to not just Indo-European but also Non-Indo-European Linguistic links. With the spread of Buddhism, Sanskrit became the religious language in many areas of the Silk Road Regions. Subsequently Buddhist texts were translated into local languages.

Similarities between Central Asian and Indian folktales abound with similar character, events and plots. There is evidence of spread over Central Asia of fairy tale plots from "Panchtantra" (3-4 A.D.), which is a collection of stories and fables in Sanskrit predating their translation into Central Asian languages. Hoja Nasruddin, the semi-mythical 'wise-fool' astride a donkey appears in folktales and Sufi teachings in Central Asia, India and other parts of the world.

Aryan, Zoroastrian and Hindu Beliefs

Indian Aryans and those from Persia share some common myths and beliefs such as Avicenna's belief about transmigration of souls, and the Zoroastrian belief that the Iranian, Indian and Turanious people are descendent souls of three brothers.

Ancient Sun temples exist throughout India and the Sun temple at Konark in India shows the Sun God wearing Slav boots! In parts of India, *Shashthi Puja* is an important festival in which the Sun is worshipped and red coloured sweet pancakes are cooked and eaten. The Slavs of yore in Central Asia and beyond observed a similar festival and cooked similar red pancakes. However, with the advent of Christianity and Islam though Sun worship died out, some still continue to cook the sweet red pancake on this day!

In Sogdiana, that spread over much of Uzbekistan and adjoining parts of Central Asia, great centres of arts and culture flourished between the 5th and 9th century A.D. in Afrosiab, Penjikent and Varaksha (near Samarkand and Bukhara). Archaeological findings suggest that Hindu religious practices existed along with the local religion 'Manichaism'.

Buddhism

Buddha was born in the 6th century B.C. in India and was a popular reformer, yet Buddhism did not become widely popular in India. It however flourished in China and Sri Lanka and returned to India via the Central Asian route to be absorbed back into Hinduism. As is known, it was from China Buddhism spread to Korea and Japan.

The Buddhist cave art originating in Indian caves made for meditations travelled with monks and artists to Bamiyan, Kucha, Kizil, Turfan, Dunhuang and China. Later Bamiyan and Bactria played a unique role in spreading Buddhism.

Interestingly, the Kyrgyz knew and practiced a Tibetan version of Buddhism – Lamaism (which the Tibetans had acquired directly from India) reference to which is found in the Kyrgyz epic Manas. Even today some Kyrgyz people in China practice Lamaism.

Christianity

Nestorian Christians travelled through Central Asia and remains of early Christian Monasteries can be found in Kyrgyzstan and other Central Asian Countries. According to a legend, Christ visited Kashmir. Another legend has it that he did not die after the crucifixion;

instead he travelled to India with Maria Magdelena through Central Asia. There is a grave in Chinese Xinjiang believed to be that of Maria Magdelena and a local belief that Jesus himself is buried in Kashmir where his grave is referred to as 'Takht-E-Suleiman' (Kresten, Holger; Jesus Lived in India, Penguin Books 2001). There is also a 'Takht-E-Suleiman' in Osh, Kyrgyzstan which is a hill revered by the local Muslims. This is an area requiring further research.

Arabs Links through Central Asia

The Arab Empire expanded its influence to India through Central Asia. Interacting with Indo-Aryan, Persian and Hellenic cultures produced the unique and rich Saracenic culture. While Baghdad became the centre of intellectual activity, Arab students came to the Indian University of Takshila to study medicine and mathematics. Textbooks of both were translated from the Sanskrit into Arabic. Indian physicians went to Baghdad to set up hospitals and medical schools.

The Afghan, Mongol and Turks in India

With the Afghan raiders Mahmud Ghazni (998–1030 A.D.) and Shahabuddin Ghuri, (c 1186 A.D.) — Indo-Central Asian links took the form of Islam. With Islam came new ideas that revitalized Hindu art and architecture giving birth to the Indo-Muslim Art form. Around this time lived the great Persian poet Firdausi, and the great scholar Al-Beruni who learnt Sanskrit, read Indian scriptures travelled widely and wrote his accounts in 'Tarikh-i-Hind'.

After Ghuri's death, his Turk slave Qutbuddin ruled, followed by Iltamush who had 25 commanders in his army drawn from Central Asian tribes such as Ilbary, Turki-kharkitais, and other Khipchak tribes who were natives of south Kazakhstan.

While Chengiz Khan returned from the banks of the Indus River without entering the plains of India, Temurlane, (1369 A.D.) conquered territories till Delhi. Though Temur plundered and destroyed cities that came in his way, ironically, returning he took with him the best of artisans, craftsmen and master-builders to build the monumental cities of Samarkand and Bukhara, which stand tribute to the new and distinct style of architecture and art that blossomed.

The Delhi Sultanate and Turkmen Influences

With the establishment of the Delhi Sultanate in the 13th century, and then the Sultanates of Bengal, Kashmir and the Deccan a vibrant relationship grew between India and Turkmenistan. The Turkmen played important roles in politics, administration, judiciary, military, architecture, art forms, literature, poetry, and in the growth of Sufism.

The Great Turkmen Bairam Beg Khan was the mentor of the Mughal Emperor Akbar and his son Abdul Rahim Khan-i-Khana occupies an important place in the cultural heritage of both India and Turkmenistan.

> "Sultan Mohammad Quli Qutub Shah from the Qara Qoyunlu tribe of Turkoman founded the City of Hyderabad in Deccan and was also a great poet and the author of rich collection of nearly 50000 couplets comprising ghazals...masnavis, qasidas, ruboies and fytas. He is the founder of Urdu language in Deccan which he did by blending Persian and Hindi." (Hangloo, R.L., 2000).

Indo-Muslim Art Form, Cultural and Religious Synthesis

With the growth of the Indo-Muslim art form as well as the trade links between Turkic Central Asia and India, Delhi emerged as an important cultural centre. Scientist, scholars and poets from Otyrar, Samarkand, Bukhara, Balkh and other Central Asian towns came and settled here.

During this medieval period in India, there was an all round synthesis of cultures, art, architecture, and lifestyles. The confluence of Hindu and Islamic thought gave rise to Sufism. The Sufi saints used Arabic and Persian intermixed with the colloquial to form a new language Hinduvi that was understood by both the elite and the common. The *Naqshbandi* order also traces its origins back to Bukhara (Rizvi, SAA 1983) and was later re-introduced in Central Asia in the late 17th century. While the *Bhakti* movement in India was influenced deeply by Sufism, the Indian poet-saints like Ramanand and Kabir borrowed the best from both religions and attempted to synthesize the two; another great reformer and religious leader Guru Nanak, founded the Sikh religion.

The Mughals

The *Emir* of Ferghana, Zahir-ud-din Babar came to India in 1526 A.D. and laid the foundation of the Mughal Empire. Utilizing the services of an architect from Constantinople he laid out a splendid capital in Agra yet yearned for the fruit (melon and grapes –which he possibly introduced to India), flowers and sights of his native Ferghana. As Babar himself, was fond of poetry, art and literature with him came new traditions.

There are records of exchange of diplomatic missions and gifts between the Mughals and the rulers of Bukhara and Kazakhstan to resolve political and economic-trade issues. Regular exchange of missions took place in 1572 A.D. (Hoja Altamush was ambassador of Bukhara in Akbar's court), in 1577 and in 1585-86 A.D.

Art and Architecture

The Central Asian and Indian art and architectural styles blended to form the Mughal style and reached their zenith in Shajahan's time with the *Taj Mahal*—which is not only a symbol of everlasting love but also the finest example of Central Asian - Indian art. With this, the cycle of history turned a full circle, for Shahjahan brought in architects, masons and master-craftsmen from all over Central Asia and India to construct this grand monument.

Similarly, the miniature art form that had grown as an expression of secular impulses in Central Asia influenced the Indian style of miniature paintings. And, decades later, the Mughal style of miniature painting revitalized the Bukhara school. So, "the process of mutual renewal and enrichment of the two cultures continued" (Abuseitova, MK 2004).

Urdu

As cultures and people interacted, a new language Urdu—(which is a Persianized Turkish word that means "camp") - gradually developed. Adding from various local languages, it grew producing new literary styles and a large volume of literature. The Mughal courts saw great poets and writers and the last Mughal Emperor, Bahadur Shah Zafar was an accomplished poet himself.

One name that stands out in Urdu as well as Persian literature is of Mirza Asadullah Khan Ghalib (19th c A.D.) whose ancestors hailed from Samarkand. One of the most intellectual poets and versatile genius of his time, he wrote in Urdu as well as in Central Asian Persian.

The last millennium witnessed dynasties of Muslims - the Khiljis, the Tughlaks, the Lodhis, the Surs and the Mughals—that ruled India for almost seven hundred years were all related to Central Asia in one way or the other. Along with the rulers came artists, mystics and scholars, some who only visited India and many who settled down here.

Even today the stamp of Central Asia is felt in the music, art, poetry, architecture, dresses and headgear, the cuisine and the flavours, and the sights and sounds of India.

Travelling through Central Asia, one is struck by the similarities the countries and people of this region have with India; similarities that go beyond terrain and topography.

The Silk Road: Indian Connection during British and Soviet Eras

Before Indian independence, British policy towards Russia and later towards the USSR determined the scope of Indo-Central Asian relations. India, as a British Colony became a part of the 'Great Game' of intrigue, rivalry, exploration and exploitation that was played amongst the superpowers of those times. With the partition of the Indian sub-continent, India lost most of its territories adjoining Soviet Central Asia, Afghanistan and Chinese Central Asia, which have now become a part of West Pakistan.

Till the end of the Soviet era in 1991, independent India's interactions with Central Asia were a part of the Indian policy towards the USSR. Indian leaders looked at socialism, planned and mixed economy as an answer to the challenges of industrial, technological, agricultural, economic and social backwardness, and religious dogma and as a vehicle for development and prosperity. Many agreements were signed—the most notable being the Indo-Soviet Treaty of Peace and Friendship of the 70s and there was as all round co-operation in science, technology, education, culture and art. Soviet support to India in the wars with Pakistan and in the international arena further cemented this relationship.

Indian trade with USSR increased manifold in the 1960s, 70s and 80s. India exported tea, shoes, leather goods, textiles and apparel, light consumer goods and medicines while the USSR exported and invested in heavy industry, steel, light industry, hydro electric projects, pharmaceutical industry, fertilizer industry, oil refineries and helped India build up its defence capability and infrastructure. In 1984, it was from Baikanur in Kazakhstan, that the first Indian cosmonaut Rakesh Sharma went into outer space aboard the Soyuz T-11 spacecraft.

Indian cinema became very popular all over Central Asia with Raj Kapoor, Mithun Chakravarty and Amitabh Bachchan becoming household names. The Soviet Union and socialism became recurrent themes in Indian cinema and literature and there was intense activity of translating Soviet works in Hindi, Urdu and other Indian languages and vice-versa. Regular exchanges of artists, performers, writers, and cultural troupes occurred from 1960s to 80s with festivals of India held in USSR (including Central Asia) and festivals of USSR in India.

USSR opened up its Universities and institutes in Tashkent, and elsewhere to Indian students who pursued science, technology, medicine, agriculture, social sciences and humanities. While Hindi and Urdu emerged as subjects of study and research at the Institute of Oriental Studies at Tashkent, gave a special boost to the study of Buddhist excavations - also by Indian archaeologists.

In ways more than one, geography and history brought the countries closer. Friendship, ideas, ideology, goods, technology, intellectual and cultural exchange and co-operation flowed. Though Western scholars refer to the decline and non-existence of the Silk Route (essentially referring to the East-West Silk Road) during this period, it is obvious that the Indian connection of the Silk Road—the South Silk Route - flourished, though differently.

The Silk Road, India and the Independent Central Asian States

After the collapse of USSR in 1991, the five independent Central Asian States that emerged went through the expected period of turmoil. Their desire to be independent appeared to conflict with their need to seek help from Russia. And their secular nature was threatened by waves of Islamism especially in Uzbekistan and Turkmenistan. The transition from Soviet socialism to market capitalism was painful and turbulent with consequent poverty, unemployment and civil unrest. With no previous experience, or the 'democratic mindset' the metamorphosis from a 'command and control' centralized model of governance to a democratic functioning with civil society participation posed a big challenge. The propositions before the Central Asian Countries have been of 'Pan-Islamism', 'Pan-

Turkic', Pro-Russian, Pro-CIS, Pro-Chinese, Pro-Western, and 'Pro-Non Aligned'.

In this fast changing scenario, India also has had to evolve an independent policy vis-à-vis these countries, as so far its relationship was only with the USSR. It is evident that the Central Asian states are of immense strategic economic and security interest to India and India can play a critical role in their development.

As Professor P.L. Dash has observed in an article in the journal Dialogue in April-June 2002, (pages 67-82), unlike other countries bordering the Central Asian States, India is different as:

- It is respected for traditional wisdom and heritage.
- It has a history of strong ties with the Central Asian Region / States
- It is a modern parliamentary democracy with a vibrant political ethos.
- It has a non-aligned foreign policy.
- It is undergoing successful economic reforms in its own way under state control.
- It is multi-ethnic and multilingual like the Central Asian States.
- It is multi-religious, non-Islamic, yet has a Muslim population more than thrice that of Central Asia.
- It has foundations of modern science, technology, academics and industry with a huge pool of skilled manpower.

Though initially slow, in the last decade and a half, top Indian leaders (including the Prime Minister) have visited the Central Asian States and reciprocal visits by their Presidents have taken place. There have been several exchanges and consultation of ministerial, bureaucratic and technical delegations and some joint ventures have taken off. Many agreements have been signed. Some that are common to all Central Asian States are:

Bilateral agreements—

- On education, culture, and sports.

- On economic co-operation and trade.
- On training of manpower and students by India.
- On India providing management consultancy.
- On information technology inputs by India.
- On agriculture and energy sector.
- On combating terrorism and drug trafficking.

India's Contemporary Engagement in Central Asia and India's Connect Central Asia Policy

In spite of the close links that have been and are still vaguely or 'romantically' alive in the popular psyche, it's a pity that today people in India or in Central Asia know little about the extent and depth of these links or about each other. There is very little people-to-people contact. It's time to revitalize these links. More so in view of the current global scenario where Central Asia is strategically crucial for India to counter fundamentalist-terrorism, drug trafficking, and to usher in peace, cooperation and stability in the Central and South Asian Region.

There was an announcement last year by the Indian Minister of State for External Affairs Shri E. Ahamed of India's 'Connect Central Asia' Policy, to quote the Minister, India is now looking at a "pro-active political, economic and people-to-people engagement with Central Asian countries, both individually and collectively".

No doubt, with elegant execution, the policy agenda would result in both immediate and long term mutual gains to all partners. While India would be able to address its energy, security and trade economic needs, the new alliances would help the Central Asian States access and tap India's techno-economic potential as well as intellectual property and highly skilled (professional, managerial) human capital. As the Policy aims at investing into development, utilizing raw material domestically and raising manufacturing capacities of our Central Asian neighbours, it is bound to be more welcoming and beneficial than the approach of some others who may drain the rich natural resources of the region without development of local potential, economies or human resource.

While the policy stays clear of a 'prescriptive political approach', it is evident that the Central Asian States would immensely benefit from the Indian experience in building secular, democratic, participatory-democratic institutions that are ethno-religiously tolerant and pluralistic in nature.

Building on India and the Region's historical, cultural and political connections with opportunities provided by the Connect Central Asia Policy, it is time to create new institutions of excellence in education, technology, medical sciences, management studies, legal and jurisprudence studies, as well as applied and liberal arts. These are areas where India with its wealth of experience and human resources can well participate.

In this process of connecting, the fundamental unit of connection is the person. It is the people-to-people contact and exchange that deepens and strengthens the relationships. It is necessary therefore, to further boost academic and cultural exchange programmes. While official exchange programmes continue to grow, it is essential that travel and tourism be boosted up to help connect the young, the professionals and the old as well.

While the desire to address these issues is there, a more concerted effort is fast required. As official barriers are eased, what one needs to do is to re-establish the process of recreating India in the popular psyche of Central Asia as well as bring in Central Asia into the Indian homes and vice-versa, where it has lost space over the last two decades. What the Indian film-makers did in the era gone by, now it is the turn of thinkers, writers, artists, media persons, as well as the new world technology savvy professionals, the astute strategists, scholarly academicians, investment and trade merchants or the intrepid travelers to do so.

Silk Road Studies Programme at Jawaharlal Nehru University

To address these contemporary challenges, multidisciplinary

International Conference: Revisiting the Silk Road; Cultural Connections, Current Challenges was held at the Jawaharlal Nehru University, New Delhi in November 2012.

It was felt that with India's 'Connect Central Asia Policy' in place, what is now required is to involve all stakeholders in a Programme to build institutions and processes that promote all round cooperation through mutual participation.

Subsequently, we have established the Silk Road Studies Programme at JNU which is a broad based multidisciplinary Programme of Studies that would build on cultural and linguistic linkages to address matters of political, security, economic and cultural cooperation between India and the regions of the Silk Road.

The Programme is founded on the belief that of the various layers on which relationships between India and Central Asia as well as other countries of the Silk Road Regions can be built, the deepest and most lasting can be built through educational institutions and exchange of scholars, academicians, researchers and young persons who shall be the thought and social leaders of tomorrow.

These institution-to-institution and person-to-person connections coupled with the immense possibilities of 'virtual-connections' that today's technology offers can overcome challenges of lack of land connectivity, borders and geo-politics.

The JNU Silk Road Studies Programme aims to bring new perspectives to promoting, preserving and teaching the Silk Road Regions' languages, cultures, philosophies and history along with science, technology, and management to create new repositories of knowledge and wealth of human capital, benefiting and bringing the people of the region closer; shaping policy to strengthen relationships and mutual exchange, as well as enhancing cooperation, peace and stability in the region and beyond.

The activities of the Programme would cover the Central Asia and Caucasian regions, as well as those of the Indian Subcontinent and adjoining areas, that form the regions of the Silk Road. These would serve the needs of students, scholars and academicians; analysts, development and policy experts, industrial and business enterprises, the media, as well as other agencies. It would work to strengthen people to people contact as well as identifying and building new areas of collaboration.

Domains of Work

The key domains of the interdisciplinary include:

- Language Studies
- Culture Studies
- History and Civilization Studies
- International Relations and Geopolitics
- Economic Cooperation, Trade and Commerce
- Defence and Strategic Studies
- Development Studies

Proposed Activities

Key modalities of working of the JNU Silk Road Studies Programme include:

- Establishing national and international institutional partnerships
- Initiating interdisciplinary new teaching and training programmes including short term and regular programmes of studies
- Founding programmes of research
- Formulating policy recommendations
- A publications programme to bring in public domain research at JNU as well as that of our research partners through a newsletter, journal and web publications
- Establishing a library and documentation unit
- Conducting seminars, workshops and conferences
- Conducting lectures for academia, as well as public

- Initiating and participating in Cultural and Academic Exchange Programmes
- Instituting fellowships and awards

The Programme proposes to use the latest teaching technologies such as video-conferencing with institutions and experts abroad or in other parts of India, webinars, online academic inputs, web resources etc.

The JNU Silk Road Studies Programme has received all round support from friends in the Central Asian Regions. It already has proposals to teach the Kyrgyz language and Azerbaijani and other proposals are being invited. Research proposals including one to study the extinct ancient Indic script *Kharosthi* which was used in Gandhara and Bactria and as far as Khotan and Nisa have been received.

The ancient and the traditional cultural links provide the backdrop to the current drama of international exchange, the intricate socio-cultural fabric into which can be woven new patterns of peace and understanding to face global challenges together.

While the Central Asian countries offer oil, gas, and natural resources; emerging markets and investment opportunities, they are strategically important from the Indian perspective for other reasons too. India has much to offer to the Central Asian States in terms of building democratic institutions, stability, economic and social development, defence and anti-terrorist training, information technology, management as well as other inputs.

Just as we mortals are bound to our historical, socio-cultural and genetic destinies, the Indian and Central Asian regions are bound by common geo-history, culture and gene pool, and so bound in destiny.

It is imperative therefore, to rejuvenate the flow of culture, commerce and common-contact along the Silk Road Routes to help move towards a progressive and stable Central and South Asian Region.

So, to conclude, as we cross the 20th anniversary of the establishment of diplomatic ties between India and the Central Asian States, it is time for us to look at the whole Central Asian Region and the India Sub-continent as 'Common Culture Region' and work towards reviving and re-establishing the bonds of people to people folk and common culture to weave a new tapestry of peace, progress and harmony. For this has bearing on all the regions of the erstwhile Silk Road.

One may conclude by saying that, the reality and significance of the Silk Road exists even today. Turkmenistan and India have so much in common and their destinies have been linked together since antiquity, they can achieve so much by being together particularly when we talk about neutrality and peace.

Turkmenistan's Neutrality Status and its Contribution to Peace and Development

Nirmala Joshi

It was a historic decision by the Turkmen leadership to opt for 'Neutrality Status' for the fledgling state, when it gained unexpected independence in 1991. The breakup of the Soviet Union left all the post Soviet states unprepared for this sudden dissolution. The immediate priority for Turkmenistan was the security and stability of the country, as well as the safety and well being of its citizens. Turkmenistan faced an enormous challenge as it wanted to re-build a new socio, political and economic policy and at the same time dismantle the old system, and most importantly Turkmenistan wanted to build a nation-state with a Turkmen identity. It was a gigantic task in the absence of requisite experience and expertise.

Nevertheless, in spite of all the odds work on rebuilding had to start. And hence domestic stability became absolutely essential. In the perception of the Turkmen leadership a neutral state would be able to guarantee stability. As a consequence on 9-10 July 1992 Turkmenistan declared neutrality, as the guiding principle in foreign policy. Possibly Turkmenistan apprehended interference in its affairs from external sources. However, Turkmen concept of neutrality did not denote an isolationist approach to foreign policy. It was a positive concept. Its essence lay in avoiding Bloc politics, alliances and groupings. Cooperation and Peacemaking were the hallmarks of the concept and not competition; Turkmenistan wanted to play a role at the regional and global level within the framework of the United Nations (UN) or its specialized agencies. At the domestic level the leadership wanted to find their answers and solutions to the nation building process.

Inspired by the ideals of Non Aligned Movement (NAM) Turkmenistan declared its intention to join it and at the Cartagena summit formally became a Member (October 1995). Subsequently, Turkmenistan's request for 'Permanent Neutrality of Turkmenistan' was granted by the United Nations General Assembly (UNGA) and a resolution was passed to the effect on 12th December 1995. For Turkmenistan this recognition by the UN was important, because it does not impose any constraints on a country, and enjoys high degree of international authority. The major features of positive neutrality were respect for the sovereignty and territorial integrity, non interference in internal affairs, non use of force in international relations and priority of the UN decisions in international affairs.

Stability and Peacemaking

Turkmenistan's concept of neutrality did not denote an isolationist approach, rather an active one. The Guiding Principles of its foreign policy lay in cooperation and peacemaking. With the beginning of Afghanistan's emergence as the epicenter of radicalism and the beginning of the 'war on terror' the Turkmen meaning of stability widened to include regional security as well. The beginning of the Tajik civil war and the refuge the Tajik Opposition received in Afghanistan is a case in point. The Central Asian Republics (CARs) are in the midst of their transformation process and need stability and peace for development. Moreover the potential for conflicts in the Central Asian region is strong particularly ethnic conflicts. The issue of sharing the waters of trans-boundary rivers or the border settlement especially in the Fergana valley or the environmental degradation soon acquired an ethnic colour. Besides, the role of major powers in Central Asia exacerbated some of these tensions.

In view of Turkmenistan's core foreign policy principle of Neutrality the UN opened its Regional Center for Preventive Diplomacy in Central Asia in Ashgabat in 2007. The aim of the Centre was to provide a platform to the CARs within the UN framework to discuss all divisive and contentious issues before they could spiral into a potential source of conflict. In order to enlarge the peace agenda Turkmenistan organized a conference at Dushanbe in 2008 to debate and deliberate upon the most divisive issue - sharing of the waters of the trans-boundary rivers. Though the conference could not arrive at consensus, it nevertheless gave an opportunity to the leaders to express their respective points of view. Similarly Turkmenistan had offered to organize a conference on a similar pattern to discuss the Afghan developments.

In accordance with its foreign policy goals Turkmenistan organized the first Summit of Head of States of Caspian States. President Gurbanguly Berdimuhamedov has also offered to organize a conference on 'Disarmament in Central Asia and the Caspian Sea Basin'. In this regard Turkmenistan is ready to establish the 'Inter Regional Center on Disarmament in Asia'. Turkmenistan is a signatory to the Semipalaytinsk Treaty of making Central Asia a Nuclear Weapon Free Zone. The issue of environmental degradation is also acquiring serious proportions; with the shrinking of the Aral Sea and the two perennial rivers, and the increasing desertification in Central Asia, Turkmenistan has suggested the creation of an Inter-Regional Center to address the issue of climate change. It has also offered to convene a 'Forum on Security and Peace' in the Central Asian region. In short, Turkmenistan has offered to work within the framework of its neutrality status for peace and stability on all issues that are of regional as well as global significance.

Issues of Economic Development

The transformational process in Turkmenistan is going on; it would like to develop rapidly and integrate with the world economy. Turkmenistan has two major economic assets—energy resources and its favourable geopolitical location. Turkmenistan is the fifth largest depository of natural gas in the world and new finds could raise this position. Due to its geographical location Turkmenistan can connect with the east, west, north and south. Overland transport connectivity is essential, as the countries of the region are landlocked.

Energy Resources

At the time of independence there was one natural gas pipeline linking it with Russia. Being landlocked Turkmenistan faces the problem of transporting gas to world markets. It has to depend on the good will of third countries. An additional problem is that Turkmenistan is located in a region that is rich in natural gas - Russia in the north and Iran in the south. In fact Russia was undercutting Turkmen gas by offering prices lower than the international ones. The pricing issue is a vexatious one causing periodic strains in the relationship. That is why perhaps President Saparmurat Niyazov opted for a neutrality status so that Turkmenistan could minimize the uncertainties and maximize its sales to other markets. At present there are two pipelines going to China, and two more are in the planning stages other than the one going to Russia. There is a short pipeline, the Kopezhe-Kurt Kui pipeline going to northern Iran.

Viewing this problem as a global challenge, an integral part of global security Turkmenistan introduced a resolution in the United Nations General Assembly (UNGA) "Reliable and Stable Transit of Energy Resources and its Role in Sustainable Development and International Cooperation". Hopefully, the Resolution would fill a vitally needed gap that compels landlocked countries to depend on the political will of third countries for energy transit. It should lead to a universally recognized legal framework for agreement on guarantees for uninterrupted transit of energy. The important thing is that the Resolution is a harbinger of a new approach; from competition to cooperation. Subsequently, an international conference was held in Ashgabat to discuss this issue in April 2009. An expert group was constituted to frame the requisite legal framework for adoption by the UNGA. It is not clear whether the framework agreement is ready or not. However, a Resolution of such a nature would brighten the prospect for the much awaited Turkmenistan-Afghanistan-Pakistan-India (TAPI) pipeline to get operationalized. The TAPI project was slowly, but surely inching forward. Operationalization of TAPI would also brighten the prospect of reviving the ancient trade route from the Indian subcontinent.

Transport Corridors

Ever since President Berdimuhamedov assumed the Presidency in 2007, he has vigorously pursued the idea of making Turkmenistan the hub of overland rail/road transport sector. Interconnectedness is crucial for economic development, as it helps landlocked countries to reach out to world markets. In fact the ancient trade route from the Indian subcontinent passed via Turkmenistan; one branch going westwards via Dehistan towards the Caspii region and one going in the southern direction towards Persia. The fabled Silk Route passed through Turkmenistan's city of Merv which was an important junction on this route.

Consequently President Berdimuhamedov's first trip abroad was to Iran. The aim was to firm up rail projects, and enhance connectivity between the CARs and the Persian Gulf. The President also undertook a similar trip to Afghanistan. During his visit he proposed a rail link between Turkmenistan and Afghanistan. This link is now operational, and has helped Turkmenistan to render humanitarian assistance to Afghanistan's north western provinces. In December 2014 a highly prestigious rail project connecting Kazakhstan-Turkmenistan-Iran was inaugurated in the presence of the three Presidents. Apart from transporting bulk cargo and goods at a faster pace, the physical infrastructure that has come up along the route will promote economic development. The International North South Transport

Corridor linking India via Iran to Russia also stands to benefit by this rail link. Another project that is in the construction stage is the Turkmenistan-Afghanistan-Tajikistan rail project. Probably this project is awaiting investments. But as and when completed Kyrgyzstan could also join it. Meanwhile Turkmenistan is also improving rail/road links between the main cities of its country. An equally important overland corridor worth mentioning is the Georgia-Azerbaijan-Turkmenistan-Afghanistan transport route. Hopefully this corridor would be extended to Pakistan and India.

In order to strengthen the geo-economic component of its neutrality, Turkmenistan has initiated a Resolution in the UNGA 'Role of Transport and Transit Corridors in ensuring International Cooperation for Sustainable Development'. The Resolution was adopted by consensus in December 2014. Earlier in September 2014 a major international conference was held in Ashgabat to deliberate upon the issue of transport corridors. The conference discussed at length all the aspects of the Resolution and at the end issued the 'Ashgabat Declaration'. Among the various points of the Declaration the following point needs to be mentioned:

> Agreed to continue to accord priority to develop, operationalize and take measures to improve infrastructure and facilities, facilitate cross border transport and customs clearance along the international, regional and inter regional transit transport corridors.

Turkmen efforts in the energy and transport sector sum up the essence of neutrality.

India and Turkmenistan have had civilizational ties, and throughout the histories of the two countries cultural contacts have been maintained. India is supportive of Turkmen foreign policy and its crux 'The Neutrality Status'. India has also accorded high priority to connectivity with Afghanistan and Central Asia. The opportunity for India and Turkmenistan to cooperate in both the energy and transport sector has opened up. India could also cooperate in the physical development of these projects.

Concluding Observations

Turkmenistan's policy of neutrality is playing a positive role in broadening the area of peace and stability so vitally needed in a region that is in turmoil. Turkmenistan will continue with its efforts at peacemaking, as its policy slogan is "*All problems have a solution, nothing is impossible*".

History of Neutrality and its Current Application

Amangeldi Rahmanov

The year 2015 was special as Turkmenistan along with the global community had celebrated the historical event—the 20th Anniversary of international recognition of the permanent neutrality of Turkmenistan. As a result of the initiative taken by the Esteemed President of Turkmenistan Gurbanguly Berdimuhamedov, 2015 was announced as the "Year of Neutrality and Peace".

The year 2015 was also the 20th Anniversary of Turkmenistan's membership at the Non-Aligned Movement (NAM). And this book is a significant part of a year-long celebrations, events, and activities and has a great importance to this effect.

In this connection, it is important to briefly dwell upon the history of Neutrality of Turkmenistan and its relevance to the modern days.

Turkmenistan was part of the former Union of the Soviet Socialist Republics, and with its disintegration Turkmenistan became an independent state. The state has adopted its own policy of permanent and positive neutrality on the basis of noble traditions of its people. At the same time, the fundamental provisions of this neutral policy were formulated by its people. These are—peace, non-interference in the affairs of other states, respect for their sovereignty and territorial integrity, mutually beneficial relations, mutual respect, non-participation in international military organizations and treaties, resolution of international issues through political and diplomatic means.

The Government thought that only such kind of a policy will suit its national interest, allow its people to live in peace and harmony with neighbours, maintain and develop friendly and equal relations with all the countries of the world.

After having made a choice in favour of Policy of Permanent Neutrality, government of Turkmenistan wanted to get recognition of its Neutral Status by the United Nations. And it was the single priority task of the foreign policy and diplomacy of Turkmenistan at that period of time.

Thus, on December 12th, 1995, the United Nations General Assembly (UNGA) on its 50th jubilee session adopted the Resolution Number 50/80 with the title *Permanent Neutrality of Turkmenistan.* By doing so the UNGA supported the permanent neutral status of Turkmenistan, while expressing hope that Turkmenistan's permanent neutrality status would contribute to strengthening of peace and security in the region. Adoption of this legally binding significant document by the United Nations General Assembly meant that the international community recognizes Turkmenistan as a Neutral State, supports its Neutral Policy and further improves its international-legal basis.

As per Turkmenistan it is the first country to get its neutrality recognized by the United Nations.

The other features are:

- It reflects the history of the country, contemporary internal conditions of Turkmenistan, its geographical and geopolitical situation and the noble traditions of Turkmen people;
- Turkmenistan's neutrality is recognized and confirmed by the Resolution of the United Nations General Assembly as

the "Permanent Neutrality of Turkmenistan" and by other documents;

- Turkmenistan's neutrality is permanent by form, that is unlimited by time and valid in wartime as well as in peace;
- Turkmenistan's neutrality is positive and constructive, which implies the state's active role in matters related to maintaining peace and stability, developing friendly relations and cooperation among states.

Turkmenistan builds mutually beneficial and friendly bilateral relations with all the states. At the same time, its neutral status gives special dynamism to the country's international relations: today Turkmenistan is a member of 132 International Conventions and Treaties, which vividly confirms strengthening of international recognition of its foreign policy and activities. At present Turkmenistan has established diplomatic relations with 134 countries, and is member of 44 International Inter-governmental Organisations.

The main foreign policy of Turkmenistan remains the same—strengthening of global and regional peace, security and stability. The main focus is on the efforts at the regional level.

Turkmenistan plays an active role in resolving critical regional and global issues, puts forward comprehensive foreign policy initiatives aimed at maintaining the peace, security and sustainable development. For example, at the 69th Session of the UN General Assembly Turkmenistan proposed a number of new initiatives in such areas, as Global Peace and Security; Energy Security; Development of Cooperation in the Field of Transport; Humanitarian Issues; Ecology and Climate Change, which was supported by other nations too.

The neutral policy of Turkmenistan also has a large peace-making potential. Particularly, in the 1990^{s} Turkmenistan played important role in conducting negotiations towards settling the situation in Afghanistan, as well as the peaceful settlement of a civil conflict in Tajikistan.

Such areas as trade, commerce, culture and environment are also getting their due attention in Turkmenistan's foreign policy aimed at developing cooperation with other nations. For example, today Turkmenistan maintains trade and economic relations with more than 100 countries; while favourable investment climate in the country resulted in Turkmenistan getting placed in the first ten countries on the index of attraction of Direct Foreign Investments in 2012.

Although the foreign policy of neutral Turkmenistan is an evolving process, it is based on scientifically devised mid-term document—which is the "Foreign Policy Concept of Turkmenistan for the Years 2013-2017".

In short, practical and successful implementation of domestic and foreign policies of Turkmenistan shows that the potential and perspectives of neutrality are virtually unlimited. Turkmenistan's experience of development also indicates that neutral policy appeals to the national interests ofTurkmenistan the most, while it has become a real instrument of mutual understanding and cooperation among nations.

The origins of friendly, historical and cultural ties, common spiritual values of Turkmen and Indian people lie in the depth of millennia. Following the principles of permanent neutrality, Turkmenistan attaches great importance to strengthening of the Turkmen-Indian friendship and developing bilateral cooperation. Today, in a new historical epoch, traditional ties of friendship and cooperation between people of Turkmenistan and India have got a new dynamism in political, diplomatic, economic and other spheres.

It is well known today that energy security becomes an important factor for not only individual countries but also at the regional and global scale, regardless of the level of development. And, as an energy power house, Turkmenistan based on traditions of permanent neutrality actively involves itself in the process of forming of new approaches aimed at resolving the issues of energy security in Eurasian continent.

Turkmenistan also considers transport and communication sector as an important factor in developing of inter-regional relations in the long term, as well as the creation of infrastructure in the new geo-economic space.

Turkmenistan's efforts and initiatives paid off in the form of adoption of two resolutions by the United Nations General Assembly in 2008 and 2013, titled "Reliable and Stable Transit of Energy and its Role in Ensuring Sustainable Development and International Cooperation". These Resolutions paved the way for the International Expert Group to hold its first meeting in Ashgabat in December, 2014. The main task of this Group was to prepare a draft Convention on Energy Security.

On December 19, 2014, the United Nations General Assembly adopted yet another Resolution "Role of Transport and Transit Corridors in Ensuring International Cooperation for Sustainable Development", initiated by Turkmenistan. Resolution calls on Member-States of the United Nations, International and Regional Organisations to start and intensify cooperation on transport. Turkmenistan is grateful to India for its support which was provided for its international initiatives at the UN General Assembly Sessions and on other high level forums.

At the same time, Turkmenistan considers India as a strategic partner in the energy sector. In this context, India as one of the participants of Turkmenistan-Afghanistan-Pakistan-India (TAPI) 1735 km Gas Pipeline Project, is also interested in actively promoting this project, which will deliver 33 billion cubic meters of natural gas per year to these countries. The Project aims to make a significant contribution to the sustainable socio-economic development of the countries of Central and South Asia and the Asian region as a whole.

Turkmenistan and India have also established reliable air transport connectivity while at the same time mutually beneficial cooperation in the field of land transportation with the opening of the North-South Rail Corridor through Turkmenistan which has a tremendous potential for boosting bilateral trade and has a bright future.

At the outset, it should be highlighted that this historical event that the people are witnessing is a history in itself in the making,—symbolizes the strict adherence of Turkmenistan and Turkmen people to loving peace, creativity and principles of universal humanism and brotherhood.

India and Turkmenistan: Way Ahead

Mohammed Afzal

The year of 2015 marked the milestone event in the history of modern Turkmenistan.

Honourable President of Turkmenistan Mr. Gurbanguly Berdimuhamedov has rightly noted that in the context of the historical development of Turkmenistan's Neutral Status, the Non-Aligned Movement has played a special role. At the Summit in Cartagena in October 19, 1995, Turkmenistan joined the Non-Aligned Movement and on December 12, 1995, the General Assembly of the United Nations Organization had passed special resolution 'On Neutrality of Turkmenistan'.

2015 was a milestone year in the history of modern Turkmenistan as it marked two special events: the 20th Anniversary of the unanimous recognition of the International legal status of Permanent Neutrality of Turkmenistan by the UN as well as the 20th anniversary of its membership of the Non-Aligned Movement. Honourable President and the Council of Elders of Turkmenistan have declared 2015 as the 'Year of Neutrality and Peace'. Year-long celebrations culminating in a Global Summit of Heads of States as well as Secretaries General of the UN, OSCE, CIS, ECO, OIC, NAM, SCO[1]

1. Abbreviations: UN – The United Nations; OSCE – Organization for Security and Cooperation in Europe; CIS – Commonwealth of Independent States; ECO – Economic Cooperation Organization; OIC – Organization of Islamic Cooperation; NAM – Non-Aligned Movement; SCO – Shanghai Cooperation Organization.

and other international organizations was held at Ashgabat on 12 December 2015 for a dialogue on global peace, security and development.

Forming an extended neighborhood, India and the regions of the Silk Road have had links that predate history. The close cultural, linguistic, ethnic, trade and geo-political exchanges between the Turkmen people and India that grew over the last two millennia continue to tie modern India and Turkmenistan in inseparable historic destinies. India as a founding architect of the Non-Aligned Movement and an advocate of world peace and international cooperation has a leading role in building regional security and development. Inter alia these, with 'positive neutrality' as the core of Turkmenistan's foreign policy, and India's 'Connect Central Asia Policy' the ties between India and Turkmenistan stand poised for new dimensions of economic, political, cultural, natural resource, and strategic cooperation.

The majority of Indians may know a lot about Central Asia, but only a few from among them visit this area frequently, when compared to their visits to other countries. There is a great similarity between the cultures and linguistic heritage of India and Turkmenistan. There are many common words in Hindi/Urdu and Turkmen languages. There are common words like: *Aasman* (sky), *Kursi* (Chair), *Purdah* (veil), *Chapati* (Indian bread), *Ajab* (wonderful), *Aql* (wisdom), *Ashiq* (lover), *Awaz* (sound), *Aina* (mirror), *Azad* (free), *Jawab* (answer), *Dost* (friend), *Dushman* (enemy), *Duniya* (world), *Dukan* (shop), *Makan* (house), *Halwa* (sweet dish), *Gunah* (sin), *Hawa* (air), *Insaan* (human being), *Maidan* (field) and *Adalat* (court) and many more. Not only this, both male and female names are also similar in both the countries. People of Turkmenistan have great respect for Indians and Indian culture. They like Indian music and have a fine taste for Indian arts.

There are numerous achievements of the diplomatic relations of the two countries. One important step in this direction is the Turkmenistan-Afghanistan-Pakistan-India (TAPI) Gas Pipe line accord. In fact, the framework for this accord was planned in 1990, but then India was not a part of it, it was only an observer in the project till 2007. However, the leadership in both the nations took a keen and mutual interest in the matter and India joined the standing committee in its 10th meeting as a full-fledged member. With this development, the project was re-titled as TAPI. After a period of two and a half years, the Agreement to this effect was signed on 11th December, 2010. This gas pipe line is 1735 km long, with 735 km in Afghanistan and 800 km in Pakistan, after which it enters India. As per an assessment, this gas pipe line would fulfill around 15 per cent of gas requirement of India. This is the biggest achievement of Indo-Turkmen diplomatic ties. It will also help all the four countries strengthen their mutual relations further. It will also help in re-constructing Afghanistan and improving Indo-Pak relations.

In the end, it would be worth mentioning that the Indo-Turkmen Friendship Society will continue to play an active role in promoting and strengthening friendly relations, between the two nations.

Neutrality and Peace

Turkmen-Indian Success in Bilateral Relationship

A.A. Burynow

Great reforms and initiatives proposed on an international level by the Esteemed President Gurbanguly Berdimuhamedov and Turkmenistan's partnership with the developed countries and international organizations were historically significant events. The Permanent Neutrality which was assigned by the United Nations twenty years ago to this powerful state will have great significance in realizing these tasks successfully. It was hoped that the year 2015 which was announced as the Year of Neutrality and Peace by the Esteemed President of Turkmenistan will bring success not only to Turkmen nation but also to all the countries in the world; specially to those countries that had been in close contact with Turkmenistan since ages and to those that have good relations with Turkmenistan now.

There are numerous episodes in history where the fates of Turkmen and Indian nations have intertwined. These episodes were noted down by the mediaeval chronicles. It is significant to note that the first appearance of Turkmens in India is due to the establishment of Kushan Empire in I-IV centuries AD in Central Asia, Afghanistan, Pakistan and North India. Moreover, the evidence of ancient multilateral relations of these two nations can be found in the museums of Turkmenistan and India.

Great sons of Turkmenistan like the magnificent statesman and commander, genius and talented connoisseur of Oriental literature Bairam Khan Turkmen and his son who was one of the ministers of Great Mogul Empire, the capable commander and gifted translator—poet Abdul Rahim Khan-i-Khana who wrote glorious pages in Indian history are some such Turkmen people who came and settled in India. Turkmen people are glad to know that Indian people respect and value their heritage. The great Turkmen poet Magtymguly Pyragy had mentioned in his poetry that he visited North India and he expressed his well-intentional impressions of this country in his poetry. It would not be an exaggeration to say that these two nations have always been in close contact with each-other.

Architectural symbols of these two nations like The Gate Hinduwan which is situated in one of the most ancient and most powerful states of mediaeval Turkmenistan; Turkmen Gate, which was built in the centre of the capital of India; Qutab Minar (Tower) in Delhi and Kutlug-Timur Tower in Koneurgench resemble each other very much. The vital issues nowadays are to make significant contributions to the world by these two nations and to further develop the ancient relationship of these two countries in the XXI century. That is why the Esteemed President of Turkmenistan attaches great importance in improving equitable and mutually beneficial relationship in every field as a principal course of state policy. In recent years meetings and conferences were frequently organized by these two nations which created suitable conditions for the growth of trade and industry and culture and humanitarianism.

The Esteemed President of Turkmenistan made a state visit to the Republic of India on 24-26th of May in 2010 to heighten the levels of relationship between the two leaders.

It was emphasized during this visit that India is one of Turkmenistan's strategic partners. For this very reason the Esteemed President of Turkmenistan strived for developing Turkmen-Indian contacts multilaterally and rapidly since his very first days as a leader of the state. As a result, bilaterally beneficial relations between these two countries advanced at a strong pace. According to the information which was mentioned in the beginning of that visit, the trade turnover between two states was twenty percent higher than in 2008.

There are dozens of enterprises in Turkmenistan that function with the Indian investment and a number of projects and contracts that are carried out by Indian companies. There is a pharmaceutical company by the name of "Turkmenderman Ajanta Pharma Limited" which is one of the largest enterprises in Turkmenistan which is a solid example of collaboration of Turkmenistan with India.

The hearty welcome of the President of Turkmenistan on the sacred land of India by Indian people showed that India is willing to take the ancient brotherhood ties with Turkmenistan to a new level in the new historical epoch. High-executive talks were held between the states that account for one fifth of the world population and during these talks the two countries discussed vital issues of broadening contacts and cooperation. During these talks, both sides expressed their intention of developing the trade and industry and oil and energy branches and also developing the fields of machinery and communication and humanitarian systems.

India expressed a special interest in building the Turkmenistan-Afghanistan-Pakistan-India (TAPI) pipeline, which will open up great opportunities for bringing natural gas from Turkmenistan to the international market. The implementation of this grand project worked out by the Esteemed President of Turkmenistan will not only satiate the necessity for this valuable fuel, but also will create perspectives for smart growth in Asian continent.

Attention was paid to the establishment of overhead trackage between the two sides for the development of cooperation in the sphere of transport and communication as it will undoubtedly give an opportunity for India to enter the markets in the regions of CIS[1] and the Caucasus. Moreover these routes will create favourable conditions for European countries to market their products in India.

1. CIS – Commonwealth of Independent States.

One of the main subjects discussed at the meeting was to develop cooperation in cultural and humanitarian fields. This was the continuation of old friendly relations of the two countries. During the talks it was mentioned that there was an opportunity to learn Indian language at the Institute of World Languages named after Dovletmammet Azady. It was also suggested that a special department should be created where Urdu language could be learnt and to create an information centre to assimilate high technology.

Not only were the bilateral issues discussed during the talks but also the issue of combining the efforts of the two nations to contribute to the United Nations' Non-interference Movement and including other nations in this significant task. The sides agreed that their principal aim is to fight terrorism and illegal drug trafficking. The Agreements and Contracts that were signed showed the success of the first visit of the President of Turkmenistan to India.

As a result of these negotiations such documents as an agreement between Turkmen government and Indian Republic about freeing the diplomatic passport owners from disposal demands; a plan about educational cooperation between Turkmenistan and India; an agreement between Turkmen government and Indian Republic about trade and economic cooperation; an agreement between Turkmen government and Indian Republic about educational and technological cooperation; a cooperation plan about education, knowledge, culture, art, tourism, sport and mass media between Turkmenistan and India for 2010-2012 were finalized which are the proof of favourable bilateral cooperation between these two countries.

The first visit of the Esteemed President of Turkmenistan to Indian Republic gave an opportunity to realize that behind the desire of strong co-operation and friendly relationship lays a relationship of many centuries. The most important activities of the first visit of The President of Turkmenistan to India were the visit to the tomb of Abdul Rahim Khan-i-Khana who was one of the early statesmen of Turkmen-Indian friendly relationship and a government official who gained India's love; a visit to the tomb of the great East scholar and a man of letters Bairam Khan Turkmen, first floor of which was built in 1199, but later was rebuilt by Turkmen Sultan Qutubuddin Aibek up to a height of 72.6 meters which is known in India as '*Qutab-Minar*', which is the highest tower in India and the highest brick tower in the world; his visit to the sacred '*Kuwwat ul Islam*' mosque; his visit to Mahatma Gandhi's cremation site and his visit to the *Taj Mahal*, which is considered to be one of the seven wonders of the world. This visit is talked about by the Turkmen people with great pride.

One of the important events that showed the urgency to develop cordial relationships between two nations as was being maintained by the older generations of these two countries was the publication of the book titled '*Ahalteke horses - our pride and fame*' written by the Esteemed President of Turkmenistan. This book was presented in Indian language at a function which was held at hotel 'Taj Palace' in India. The keen interest shown by the participants in this function and also in other exhibitions of the wonderful books of the President of Turkmenistan once again displayed the strong relationship between these two nations since ancient times and their desire to a stronger relationship in a new historical age.

The Esteemed President of Turkmenistan pays a great deal of attention to humanitarian cooperation that will encourage two friendly nations to strengthen their relationship in future. In recent years, the Turkmen-Indian cultural relations have been active. Indian artists and groups have come for concerts in Ashgabat several times. Showing of Indian films became a tradition in Turkmenistan. An Indian film show was held in Mary city on the 30th of March, 2014. Indian scientists and artists and intelligentsia actively participate in international level conferences, festivals and exhibitions held in Turkmenistan.

Artists from Turkmenistan often visit India and attend varied international meetings, exhibitions and symposiums. Turkmen—Indian Information Technologies Center has been established at the Turkmen State University named after Magtymguly Pyragy. There is an International Day of Indian language held in Turkmenistan. Indian language specialists are trained at the Turkmen National Institute of World Languages named after Dowletmammet Azadi.

The activities of the Indian—Turkmen Friendship Society increase the cooperation and friendship in the humanitarian field. A lot of activities in the cultural field that are organized by the Ministry of Culture of Turkmenistan and The Embassy of Indian Republic in Turkmenistan together with the Indian cultural center at the Embassy are done with the intention of strengthening close relationship of the two nations.

The main purpose of the perceptible work which was achieved in 2015—the year of Neutrality and Peace, which is the 20th anniversary of the status of Permanent Neutrality of Turkmenistan under the leadership of its Esteemed President are creating a close relationship with all the nations of the world, supporting the unity of all the people, the implementation of total security and standardized development.

Turkmenistan Celebrates 2015

The Year of Neutrality and Peace

R.N. Anil

It is a very thoughtful initiative by His Excellency Mr. Parakhat Durdyev, Ambassador of Turkmenistan to India and of the Silk Road Studies Programme of Jawaharlal Nehru University, New Delhi to publish this important book of articles "*Cooperation for Peace and Development in the Silk Road Region—India and Turkmenistan: 2015 - Year of Neutrality and Peace*".

The year 2015 was celebrated in Turkmenistan as the Jubilee Year for the recognition of its permanent neutrality status by the United Nations Organization. Incidentally, Turkmenistan had also celebrated the 20th Anniversary of its membership in the Non-Aligned Movement.

It was on December 12, 1995 when the United Nations General Assembly, for the first time in its history, adopted a Special Resolution on the Permanent Neutrality of Turkmenistan. Since then Turkmenistan's neutrality has become a phenomenon in international relations.

The main component of this policy, like India's Panchsheel[1], is the respect for sovereignty and territorial integrity of other nations,

1. Panchsheel is India's Foreign Policy based on Five Principles of Peaceful Coexistence

peaceful coexistence, non interference in other nation's internal affairs, non-use of force while settling international disputes and seeking the intervention of United Nations in solving regional and international conflicts.

Turkmenistan's model of neutrality will certainly give a comprehensive support to political stability and security to many countries around the globe. Policy of neutrality, in fact, has become an integral part and important factor in the regional and global sustainable development and has set new trends in international relations.

Today, Turkmenistan, under the astute leadership of President Gurbanguly Berdimuhamedov is marching ahead with its reformist policies of socio-political and economic developments and universal values of centuries old Turkmen tradition of peaceful coexistence, good neighbourliness and cooperation.

While summarizing the results of 2014, President Gurbanguly Berdimuhamedov says, "*We have to effectively use all the available resources—the geopolitical locations and policies of our country, based on the principles of positive neutrality, utilizing them for the peaceful resolution of conflicts through cooperation with the United Nations. Together with this leading international organization we should all put our efforts to ensure energy security, developing transport corridors and formation of a new culture*".

Positive initiatives of President Gurbanguly Berdimuhamedov, says a political commentator, have set a new agenda in international relations, such as development of global energy sector and creation of trans-continental trade, economic, transport and communication corridors that require long term projections and corresponding innovative and highly responsible decisions.

In fact, throughout the post Soviet era, Turkmenistan has taken a neutral position on all international issues and its neutrality has become the core of its foreign policy. In May 2013, the United Nations General Assembly again adopted a Turkmen Draft Resolution asking for a "Reliable and Stable Transit of Energy and its role in ensuring sustainable development and international cooperation" which was co-sponsored by 70 countries.

People of India are ardent supporters of President Gurbanguly Berdimuhamedov's policy of peace and openness who fully enjoys respect and trust among the comity of nations. The Turkmen President, while recounting his policy says, "*Our policy serves the interests of millions of people, and ultimately peace and universal prosperity.*"

During Soviet era, Turkmenistan was one of the most impoverished Republics. After independence it has undergone a sea of change and is a country which is constantly evolving. The government is determined to modernize the infrastructure and raise the standards of living of the people. The country under the dynamic leadership of President Gurbanguly is on the go. He is leading the nation from upfront. New transport corridors have been built and pipelines have been laid to ease the flow of natural gas from Turkmenistan to the neighbouring countries. It is said that within the next three years Turkmenistan will become the only country in the world exporting piped natural gas in all the four directions.

President Gurbanguly Berdimuhamedov, who took over as President of Turkmenistan in 2007, after the demise of President Turkmenbashi, is not only an able administrator but a man of culture, great intellect and a writer par excellence. He brought revolutionary changes in the country which is undergoing a significant structural transformation. Today Turkmenistan has been transformed from predominantly an agrarian economy to a modern trading economy with expanding regional and global bases. It is marching into future with full conviction and determination. The government has stepped up the growth momentum by plugging the gaps in infrastructure and channeling more investments in social sectors, like health and education.

Turkmenistan has become a welfare state. Education is universal and mandatory in the country up to the secondary level. Electricity, natural gas, water and salt are subsidized for the citizens. Even the cost of petrol is less per liter.

The women in Turkmenistan enjoy equal status with the men folk and are working in all spheres of human activity. They are engineers, doctors, teachers and in business and are richly contributing to the progress of the country.

Turkmenistan is endowed with rich natural gas deposits, ranking the third largest producer of natural gas in the world, besides having sufficient oil reserves. It also boasts of being the ninth largest producer of cotton. Because of its geo-strategic location, huge gas and oil reserves and other mineral resources, Turkmenistan has always drawn attention of big powers. However, because of its neutral status it has kept itself secure from the big power rivalry.

Turkmenistan lies in the heart of Eurasian continent. Its picturesque landscape is speckled with historic monuments and caravanserais. It is a country of incredible beauty and an ideal destination for the globetrotting tourists. Travelling across the country is a wonderful experience. People are simple, friendly and hospitable.

The Unity Award for International Understanding was presented to the then President of Turkmenistan, Saparmurat Niyazov Turkmenbashi in 1995. The award was presented in an august gathering of the village elders, at Chuli, near Ashgabat.

> "*We have a Turkmen Gate in our capital, New Delhi and it is through this gate that our nine hundred million people are watching your march to progress. Now when the gate has been opened a road of friendship should be laid down between New Delhi and Ashgabat, having bridges of goodwill all the way.*" (Author).

Lauding the traditional friendly ties between India and Turkmenistan, President Turkmenbashi said, "*They need to be sustained and reinforced in the new framework of the contemporary era*".

The organization, Unity International Foundation, which is working on the age-old Indian wisdom of **Vasudhaiva Kutumbkam** (The World as a Family) strongly supports President Gurbanguly's call for a new world order based on peace and sustainable development.

An eminent Indian public figure and President of Mahatma Gandhi Institute of Education for Peace and Sustainable Development—A UNESCO initiative in India, Dr. Karan Singh, in his book '*One Man's World*' writes: "*We must remember that science and technology have now transformed our planet into a single unit. As one travels through the world, one realizes that with all the diversity of race and religion, language and ideology, cultural and social background, economic and political systems, the world is, in fact, emerging as an indivisible unit and mankind a single family. This concept of Vasudhaiva Kutumbkam is deeply embedded in our cultural traditions*".

Turkmenistan has left an impeccable imprint on India's history. Delhi Sultanates and Kutb-shahi dynasties of Golkonda built landmark structures in India. Turkmen Gate in Delhi and Khooni Bhandara—the underground water supply system built by a Turkmen architect, Abdul Rahim Khan-i-Khana, in the 17th century are fine examples of Indo-Turkmenistan architecture in those early days.

It is not only hoped but it is a surety that the two countries will pick up the threads from their age-old relationship and weave a new fabric of close and strong ties of Indo-Turkmen cooperation in the days to come.

Neutrality of Turkmenistan and Historical Origin of Turkmen-Indian Relations

Rahmanberdi Godarov

The year 2015 was the 20th year since Turkmenistan attained Neutrality status. It was approved by the General Assembly of the United Nations Organization. The foreign policy of the Turkmen state is based on its legal status of neutrality, maintenance of peace and development of friendly relations.

This principle of Neutrality gained popularity in these twenty years in Turkmenistan though it had its importance in Turkmenistan for centuries. The main objectives of the United Nations are peace and good-neighbourly relations in today's world. Turkmenistan is an ideal country for maintaining peace and security.

One of the important objectives in the foreign policy of Turkmenistan is having good relations with India in different fields because India is one of the rapidly developing countries of the world. At present, the Turkmen-Indian cooperation in economy and culture is important. The historical, cultural and spiritual commonalities, mutual respect, strengthening of friendship and cooperation are strong bases of the Turkmen-Indian cooperation.

The celebration of the Weeks of Indian Culture and Cinema in Turkmenistan, active participation of the scientists and intelligentsia in international conferences, festivals and exhibitions organized in Turkmenistan and India are proof of Turkmen-Indian cooperation.

The Indian people and their multi-ethnicity are highly regarded in Turkmenistan. A Medical Professional School, situated in the capital of Turkmenistan, the city of Ashgabat is named after India's great leader—Indira Gandhi.

The Turkmen students, who study at the Hindi Language Department of Turkmen National Institute of World Languages named after Dovletmammet Azady are keen learners of Hindi language, literature and history of India.

Last year, a function was held on the occasion of the 290th Anniversary of the Turkmen poet which was organized by the Embassy of India in Turkmenistan, the National Institute of Manuscripts of the Academy of Sciences of Turkmenistan, Indian Society for Cultural Relations, Indian-Turkmen Friendship Society, Jamia Millia Islamia State University, Kashmir State University, Jawaharlal Nehru University and the "Pamposh Construction India Pvt. Ltd" Company where the "Collected Poems" by great Turkmen thinker and poet Magtymguly Pyragy, which were translated into Urdu were presented. The book "*Akhal-Teke*" ("Horse is Our Pride and Glory") which is about Turkmen horses, which perfected themselves during millennia and turned into model of gracefulness, beauty and faithfulness in the world, written by the Esteemed President of Turkmenistan Gurbanguly Berdimuhamedov in Hindi language has become one of the most popular books among the Indian readers. It testifies to the richness of Turkmen-Indian relations.

The Turkmen-Indian relations have originated from ancient times. The Esteemed President of Turkmenistan Gurbanguly Berdimuhamedov writes this about the past of the Turkmen-Indian links: "*The common deep historical and cultural roots, taking their origin from deep antiquity, firm traditions and customs of true friendship, mutual understanding and confidence tie Turkmenistan and India*".

The linguists and anthropologists state that there were close relations between Turkmenistan and India in ancient times. The archeological complexes of the Neolithic and Bronze periods also prove it. There are typological similarities between Migar culture of India (VI millennium BC) and Jeytun culture in the South of Turkmenistan. Science testifies that there are similarities between amazing cultures of the Bronze Age as well: the Harappa civilization and Margiana civilization.

Turkmens first appeared in India with the foundation of the Kushan Kingdom in the territory of the present North India (1st-4th centuries AD). The Muizzil, Khalaches, Kutupshahs Sultanates in Delhi, Bengal and Malva and the Great Mogul Empire were founded by the Turkmen rulers in different historical periods. The big cities like Delhi, Agra, Kashmir and Jaipur turned into scientific and cultural centers of the region; libraries, madarsahs, caravanserais and palaces were built during the rules of Babur, Humayun, Akbar, Jahangir and other sultans.

Engraving on ivory, wood and metal, sculpture, art, vocal and dance art forms were developed and many of the magnificent world famous monuments were erected.

According to historical data, one of the gates of the ancient Merv is called "Hinduvan", which means "Indian Gate". Similarly, the "Turkmen Gate" erected during the Middle-Ages in the capital of India, the city of Delhi as a symbol of friendship and brotherhood amazes visitors even today.

Famous poets like Babur, Bairam Khan-i-Khana, Hysrov Dehlevi wrote their poems in Turkmen and Persian; well-known statesman Abdul Rahim Khan-i-Khana and talented poets created their verses in Turkmen, Arabic, Persian and Hindi; they strengthened literary and cultural ties and friendly and brotherly links among the Eastern people and popularized culture and art all over the world.

In general, Turkmen people are well acquainted with historical past and unique culture of the Indian people from ancient times. The Great Silk Road also linked Turkmenistan and India. According to historical data, the Indian merchants came to the bazaars of ancient Merv and Urgench for trade. The ivory articles and stone beads, discovered at the foothills of the Kopetdag Mountains in the excavations, the manuscript in *Brahmi* script of the Indian language, including 150 varaks, related to 6th-7th centuries, discovered in the territory of Turkmenistan, in the suburbs of Bayramaly city also proves it.

The existence of fairy-tales, stories and legends in Turkmen folklore, connected with India, poetic lines about India in poems of the Turkmen classic poets like Shabende, Magrupy, Kemine and Mollanepes, including verses of great thinker and poet of the East Magtymguly Pyragy, who wrote:

I aspire and dream to go to India;
I devoted my verses to the best place-India;

testify vividly that ideas about India and the Indian people take their deserving place in Turkmen folklore and classic litrature.

The scientific, educational and cultural spheres have their special place and play a particular role in the development of multi-faceted relations between these two friendly countries. It is hoped that this book will be entered in the chronicle of the Turkmen-Indian cultural relations as a significant contribution.

Let the Turkmen-Indian relations which are based on the principles of humanism, justice, peace and goodwill be forever!

Transport Corridor and Regional Cooperation

Energy and Transit Routes

India and Turkmenistan

Sanjay Deshpande

Turkmenistan has acquired great significance because of its enormous gas reserves and gas-strategic location. Turkmenistan remained a close country to the outside world for a long time: However, situation had changed after the death of Saparmurat Niyazov in 2006. Turkmenistan developed new partnership with many countries of the world and some nations of the region. Many drastic reforms were introduced at the domestic level.

After the disintegration of the Soviet Union, the independent Turkmenistan has adopted the principles of "positive neutrality" in its foreign policy. The United Nations unanimously adopted a special resolution of the General Assembly on the permanent neutrality of Turkmenistan. 'Turkmenistan's foreign policy reflected its domestic policy. Neutrality was declared to be its guiding principle and Turkmenistan remained a member of the CIS[1] in name only; in reality, it took no real part in any activity of this organization. It has refrained from joining any of the organizations that Russia has established or plans to establish. Consistent with its foreign policy, Turkmenistan has not joined the Shanghai Cooperation Organization. Niyazov attempted to limit any external influence in order to cement the status

1. CIS – Commonwealth of Independent States

of his country as an independent nation equally distant from all foreign groups and forces.

After Niyazov's death in 2006, Berdimuhamedov emerged as the country's new leader. In his tenure, change started primarily in the form of a certain amount of liberalization. The new president approved the establishment of a multiparty system, calling it "relevant" in terms of the significant changes taking place in state administration and in terms of modernizing political mechanisms and rethinking the role and place of country's social and civil institutions. Hence, "The Golden Age" proclaimed by Niyazov has given way to a more modest and realistic "Epoch of Renaissance."

India has deep historical and cultural linkages with Turkmenistan. It is very important to India for following reasons: (a) Turkmenistan's energy resources, (b) transit potential, (c) its strategic location.

Fossil fuels are the cornerstone of Turkmenistan's regime. Gas sales accounted for more than 70 percent of the country's GDP[1]. This makes Turkmenistan an important country in vast Eurasian space, although there are some differences over the exact quantum of energy reserves it does have. The authorities use gas reserves to maintain a tolerable standard of living. Gas ensures the success of regime's populist ideology. These energy reserves have maintained a high level of interest among potential buyers enabling Ashgabat to attract the investment needed to build the appropriate infrastructure. That is why today Turkmenistan has become a competition for existing and aspiring powers like Russia, the US[2], China, the EU[3], Turkey, Iran, Pakistan and India. In the current geopolitical context, Turkmenistan has adopted a pragmatic energy policy of diversification of its energy routes. Authority of the country is attempting to engage all the markets in Europe and Asia. In 2010, Turkmenistan adopted a new gas export policy which focused on cooperation with Europe, China and greater engagement with South Asia. Under this policy,

1. GDP – Gross Domestic Product
2. US – United States
3. EU – European Union

Turkmenistan plans to increase its annual production of gas from present level of 70 billion cubic meters (bcm) to 250 billion cubic meters (bcm) by 2030. It is projected that 230 billion cubic meters (bcm) out of 250 billion cubic meters (bcm) would be exported. Turkmenistan plans to export 30 (bcm) of its gas to South Asian market through Turkmenistan –Afghanistan – Pakistan – India (TAPI) pipeline. Hence, it can be argued that India along with other South Asian countries is a prominent figure in Turkmenistan's energy export map. India imports more than 2/3 of its energy resources. India's demand for natural gas for the non-power sector alone is expected to increase from 120 million cubic meters a day to 391 million cubic meters a day by 2025. This enhances Turkmenistan's importance for India in meeting its future gas demand. Ashgabat places high hopes on the TAPI project, which envisages the construction of 1735km pipeline with a capacity of 30-33 billion cubic meters to supply to Turkmenistan, Afghanistan, Pakistan and India. Along with the Chinese export routes, it has been seen as an alternative for cooperation with Russia. According to Turkmen officials, TAPI may help to stabilize the situation in Afghanistan. At the same time, however it cannot be ruled out that the gas pipeline might be used by Taliban and other extremist organizations as a means to pressure the Afghan authorities and extort money from the companies and countries that have an interest in the uninterrupted operation of the pipeline. Thus, there is a need to maintain the security of gas traffic over the pipeline that could end the contribution to the growth of a radical opposition. The project will also lead to opening new or expanding trade, electricity and transit networks across Eurasia.

This pipeline proposes to deliver gas from Turkmenistan to Pakistan and India via Afghanistan. TAPI has potential to more tightly bind Central and South Asia. The project will also lead to opening new or expanding trade, electricity and transit networks across Eurasia, enhancing the competitiveness of Central and South Asia in the global economy. It will further allow Turkmenistan and India to boost and diversify their trade and energy relations with South Asian countries, CIS and Europe.

Currently, India-Turkmen relations are below average despite their tremendous potential. There is only one joint venture—Turkmenistan-Ajanta Pharma Ltd - which started operating after the disbursement of $15 million in loans by India to Turkmenistan. Both the countries are trying to develop the relations by signing the agreements on trade, energy and technology and planning to launch a related intergovernmental commission. India seeks access to Central Asian energy reserve particularly Turkmen natural gas. The constructed pipeline carrying gas from Turkmenistan to China via Uzbekistan and Kazakhstan clearly demonstrated that India is a latecomer in the region. Hence, India has to initiate to complete the TAPI project, which will provide India with 60 percent of the 33 billion cubic meters (bcm) of gas annually. However, difficult security conditions in Afghanistan and unresolved issues between India and Pakistan may serve to encourage the launch of TAPI rather than cause its failure. Moreover, the pipeline will provide its parties more diversified energy imports and would assist with the reconstruction of Afghanistan by providing twelve thousand jobs to the Afghans and $400 million in annual transit fees to the country. TAPI will also contribute to a more competitive economic and political environment in Central Asia, providing Ashgabat with more room to maneuver vis-a-vis Russia, US, China, India and Iran, the players who plan to have a significant presence in Turkmen energy sector.

India has actively supported Turkmenistan's neutrality, India's unprecedented economic growth and Turkmenistan's search for diversification naturally entourage them to revive the TAPI project that will further bind Central and South Asia with market's across Eurasia.

In order to establish physical connectivity with this region, India has been making a slow but steady investment in infrastructure development projects in Iran and Afghanistan. In this context, Turkmenistan occupies a special geographical position by virtue of its shared borders with Kazakhstan in the north, Uzbekistan in north and north-east, Iran in the south and Afghanistan in the south-east. It is a well known fact that Turkmenistan has been at the crossroads of the trade links between the East and the West as part of the Silk Route.

The major impediment for trade between India and Central Asia has been the lack of direct land connectivity with the region. India has been trying to work out various options because Turkmenistan can serve as a gateway to Central Asia through Iran. It is connected through rail and road which can be used by India to reach out to other CARs[1]. All Central Asian Republics have adequate rail infrastructure that links their capitals and other important cities in the region allowing movement of traffic from all directions. In this respect, Iran is the shortest and most practical alternative for India for connecting it with Central Asia via Iranian ports of Bandar Abbas and Chabahar roads and other transport infrastructure which are in good condition for movement of container trucks as well as break-bulk cargo. These routes are already operational.

International North-South Transport Corridor (INSTC) is one more transit route, in which India should be an active member. This route provides for the transit of goods through Iran and the Caspian Sea to Russia and Northern Europe. This corridor has huge potential as India, Myanmar and Thailand will also be linked by it. As compared to the other routes, the INSTC is much shorter and cost effective. From India's point of view this corridor not only helps India bypass Pakistan and yet reach out to Central Asia but also enables it to transport goods at cheaper cost to European markets. The most important is the direct road link from Bandar Abbas to Sarakhs, the land border point between Iran and Turkmenistan. Traffic can smoothly move via Iranian ports to all Central Asian Republics except Tajikistan.

Turkmenistan has also emphasized the need of development of transport and communication areas in Central Asia and Caspian basin region. Hence, Turkmenistan is making hard efforts to work for enhancing connectivity in the region. Hence, it can be said that Turkmenistan could possibly be engaged to join INSTC.

---

1. CARs – Central Asian Republics

The INSTC offers a platform for improvement in Central Asia-South Asia linkages by reducing barriers and developing communications that allow each country of these two regions to grow independently achieve national economic objectives and enhance economic growth and development so that multiple countries could benefit without compromising their own national interests. Since the corridor envisions opening vast markets in India, Russia, Central Asia, Iran and Europe, the idea of Eurasia has started assuming significance. In this context, other Eurasian countries can get involved in order to have a wider economic unity, which can use this transportation corridor to their advantage.

In conclusion, these transport routes are very important for India, Iran and Central Asia. These corridors have multiple purposes. For Russia, it is an opportunity to bypass the Silk Road. Iran gains political and economic benefits from trade with Russia, Central Asia and India. India gets access to Russia, Central Asian and European markets for its goods and links to a variety of energy import sources particularly Kazak, Russian oil and Turkmen gas. Such trade and transit routes also provide a platform to cement good relationship and partnership, reduce barriers and hurdles. Opening of the transit trade and transportation route through Iran will help in providing the competitive edge required for the markets in Central Asia. India should explore various transportation networks which will help New Delhi to propel into Central Asia in the near future.

Revival of Silk Route

Turkmenistan's Involvement in Development of Transport Corridors and Regional Cooperation

Nivedita Das Kundu

The initiation of the revival of Silk Route opened the way for innovative approaches and innovative thinking. The conceptual as well as the practical challenge was to devise a new framework to create channels and mechanisms for interaction and cooperation that would accelerate economic development and widen the sphere of international relations. Within the Eurasian region—the Black Sea, the Caspian basin and Central Asia—as well as in the encircling outer rim of countries in the Far East, South Asia, Middle East and Europe, there is a wave of enthusiasm for a revival of the ancient 'Silk Roads'. The debate on the revival of the Silk Route connectivity and development of the transport corridors is mainly to improve the linkages and increase the regional cooperation and develop trade and economic relations.

Revival of the 'Silk Route' connectivity is a mega cross-border project with a number of challenges ahead. The objective is to highlight the development of transport corridors for increasing possible regional integration, exploring resource potential, accelerating connectivity and understanding the new geo-political reality. Argument given is that the development of transport infrastructure and corridors will help increase trade and commerce as well as maintain peace and prosperity in the region. The analysis is based on the hypothesis that revival of silk route and transport corridor projects may be conceptualized as interplay of at least two competing discourses i.e. discourse of regionalism and discourse of connectivity reflecting different discursive practices. The regionalism discourse is related to integration i.e. integrating Asia with Europe. Whereas, the discourse on connectivity is tied to the transport network initiatives and diversifying of the economy. The questions are mainly as such: What is the regional discourse? What is the geostrategic implication? What is the economic significance? What is the role of Turkmenistan in the development of regional transport initiative? What are the possible challenges, and so on.

The focus is on the India-Turkmenistan historical linkages further mentioning the details about the regional transport network initiative. It also highlights the Turkmenistan-Afghanistan-Pakistan-India (TAPI) gas pipeline project and the Integrated North South Transport Corridors (INSTC).

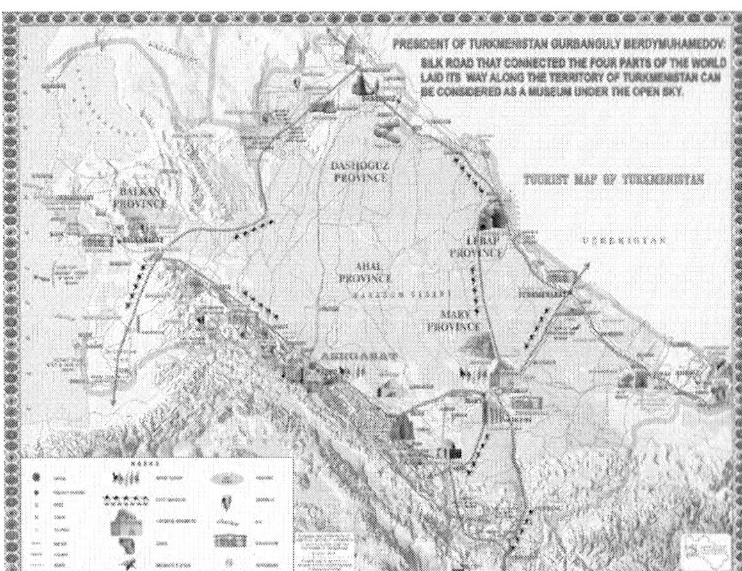

Source: Ministry of Tourism, Turkmenistan, 2013.

Map 1: Map showing Silk Route Connection with Turkmenistan

India: Turkmenistan Historical Linkages

India and Turkmenistan are closely connected with each other and share historical and civilization ties. India had close links with Turkmenistan since Kushan Empire. The territory of Turkmenistan was located at the crossroads of seven caravan routes and it became an important trade link between India, Central Asia and Europe from the very early times. India and Turkmenistan share close political understanding between each other on key regional and international issues.

Although Turkmenistan is a young state, its ties with India date back to Harappa and Indus Valley Civilizations and the Bronze Age settlements in the South and Western region of Turkmenistan such as Merv, Nisa and Dehistan. In the southern capital of Merv there are eight main Gates which are called as the Indian Gates and are still preserved along with the remnants of several caravanserais for Indian traders. Both the countries were connected through the Silk Route (i.e. the road from the Karakoram Mountains on the way towards the Khunjerab Pass or across the Hindu Kush mountains on the route towards Khyber Pass) and the relationship became close during the Silk Route trading days.

During the period of 13th-16th centuries Muhammed Bairam Khan who was the mentor of Akbar and Chief Commander of (India's) Mughal army was a Turkmen, who belonged to Baharlu Qara Qoyunlu Turkmens, also called as the Black Sheep of Turkomans, who ruled the territory of Azerbaijan, Armenia and Iraq during XIV-XV centuries. Mirza Abdul Rahim Khan-i-Khana, the famous poet and the philosopher became one of Akbar's nine prominent ministers in the Navaratnas (one out of nine gems). Another great son of Baharlu Qara Qoyunlu was Turkmen Sultan Quli-ul-Mulk, who migrated to Deccan and served under Mohammad Shah Bahmani sultan, in the middle of 16th century; later he conquered Golconda (presently in South of India) and established the Qutb Shahi dynasty in India. All eight kings of this dynasty, who ruled in Golkonda during the 171 years, were great academics. They not only patronized the economy and architecture in Hyderabad (now a South Indian city), but also contributed to the development of Persian culture, local languages and science.

In the 17th century Mughal Prince Shah Jahan built fourteen gates in New Delhi (the Capital of India), one of which was named in the honor of the Turkmen, who played a key role in the Delhi Sultanate and Mughal Empire. In Aligarh, (one of the northern cities of India) the second Turkmen Gate was built and the nearby town is still called as Turkmen Town. On the way towards the city of Aligarh one can still find the place of Bairam Khan and a well-known village of Khan-Khana which is named after Abdul Rahim Khan-i-Khana. All these factors underline the age-old linkages between India and Turkmenistan.

Regional Transport Network Initiative

Turkmenistan is actively involved in developing transport network with close regional cooperation and strong political will. Turkmenistan's geographic location makes it a significant hub for transport corridor projects connecting Asia with Europe.

In October 2007, Turkmenistan-Kazakhstan and Iran signed joint declaration for the construction of Railway line between Uzen (Kazakhstan) Kyzylkaya-Bereket-Etrek (Turkmenistan) Gorgan (Iran).

In April 2011, Turkmenistan signed intergovernmental quadripartite agreement to connect "Central Asia with Middle East" through Transport Corridor connecting Uzbekistan-Turkmenistan-Iran-Oman.

The Routes that are connecting Europe with Asia via Turkmenistan are the following:

1. Turkmenistan-Azerbaijan-Georgia (Poti Port)
2. Turkmenistan-Azerbaijan-Georgia-Turkey
3. Turkmenistan-Afghanistan-Tajikistan

The Europe-Caucasus-Asia Transport Corridor (TRACCECA) is another significant connectivity between Asia and Europe. TRACCECA Member Countries are Armenia, Azerbaijan, Georgia, Kazakhstan, Kyrgyzstan, Tajikistan, Turkmenistan, Uzbekistan, Mongolia, Ukraine, Moldavia, Turkey, Bulgaria, Romania and Iran.

Another significant project, the Turkmenistan-Uzbekistan-Tajikistan-Afghanistan-Pakistan (TUTAP) project is about the power lines connecting Turkmenistan, Uzbekistan, and Tajikistan that carries electricity to Afghanistan and possibility is that it will be connected with Pakistan and India also in near future.

Another important project of Turkmenistan: the Turkmenistan-Afghanistan-Pakistan-India (TAPI) gas pipeline project is important as it is to meet the growing energy needs of South Asia.

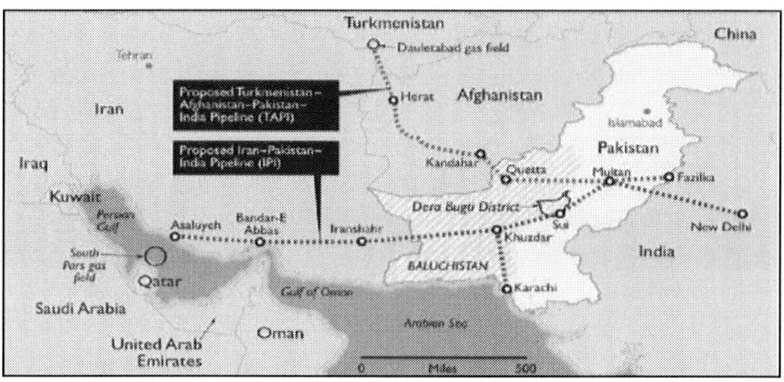

Source: Embassy of Turkmenistan, New Delhi, India.

Map 2: Map of Tukrmenistan-Afghanistan-Pakistan-India

TAPI project, proposes to deliver gas from Dauletabad gas fields of Turkmenistan to Pakistan and India via Afghanistan. Once completed, the project could change the entire region. TAPI gas pipeline project has been described by former Indian Prime Minister Dr. Manmohan Singh as the 'Pipeline of Peace'. The implementation of TAPI project will bring Central Asia and South Asia much closer in an enduring energy partnership for peace, development and prosperity for the people of the region. TAPI is expected to provide India with 60 percent of the 33 billion cubic meters (bcm) of gas annually. The Dauletabad deposits, which contain 4.5 to 16 thousand cubic meters (tcm) of gas, can supply India with the necessary volume of gas.

The TAPI pipeline starting from Turkmenistan's Dauletabad gas fields passing through Herat and Kandahar will follow Afghanistan's Ring Road. The pipeline would extend to the cities of Quetta and Multan in Pakistan and connect to the Indian city of Fazilka at the Indo-Pak border. Its total length would be approximately 1,735 km. The $10 billion TAPI pipeline's first supplies are planned for 2017. TAPI pipeline offers benefits to all four participating countries and has the potential to enhance regional cooperation. Turkmenistan, currently exports gas to Russia, Iran and China; now it will have alternative for exporting its energy resources to other countries too. South Asian countries of Pakistan and India will be able to use Turkmen gas to address their energy deficits.

The North-South Transport Corridor is another significant regional transport corridor project trying to revive the Silk Route connectivity connecting East with the West and linking the regional countries by rail, ship and even by roadways for moving freight from South Asia through Central Asia, South Caucasus and Russia to Europe. The route primarily involves moving goods from India via ship to Iran. From Iran the freight moves by ship across the Caspian Sea or by truck or rail to Southern Russia. From Russia, the goods are expected to be transported by truck or by rail along the Volga River passing through Moscow to Northern Europe. Currently, the project includes countries such as Russia, Iran, India, Kazakhstan, Kyrgyzstan, Tajikistan, Azerbaijan, Armenia, Turkey, Ukraine, Belarus and Oman, and talks are going on and it is expected that Turkmenistan will also join this project soon.

Possible Challenges

In today's world there is a growing tendency of interdependency. It has been observed that nowadays, interdependency of different social groups, states and regions has increased considerably. Today, the trans-continental transport communication increases the extent of interdependency of various States and regions and consequently enhances the degree of confidence and security and lowers the risk and conflict. It is expected that the transport corridors will increase human contacts and intensify cultural interactions. However, regional security concerns and challenges also need to be taken into consideration along with the possible economic prosperity. There will be a need to balance economic growth of various countries of the region and narrow down the discrepancy between the advanced and less developed countries. Ongoing regional conflicts pose security concerns. Any radical policy could increase the risk of chaos in the region decreasing the scope of improvement. Regional projects need to continue their progress addressing various challenges for the regional development. For better movement of goods simplifying border regulations as well as addressing customs related issues and concerns is extremely important. At present, border regulations are too stringent and there is a need to make it much simpler and faster. Visa processing also should to be much quicker for tourism and business purposes. Another very important issue that needs to be addressed is that the smaller cities and towns should also be given adequate attention along with the bigger cities. Banking procedures which are at present too complicated posing challenges for smooth trade have to be made simpler and easier to conduct the trading and commercial activities. Another challenge that is often faced is the lack of reliable news/information among the ethnic population. The language barrier remains a major issue among ethnic groups and that needs to be looked into while developing regional projects for clear understanding.

Numerous challenges appear while developing regional projects linked to transport corridors and connectivity. An integrated approach should be considered as the priority. Lack of coherence with each other's strategy and policy will not enable the development of restoring the Silk Route connections. Greater interdependency on one-another and unified objectives must be maintained and by adopting common policies the challenges can be overcome.

Future Scenarios: 2025

Here it has been sought to outline and assess the dynamics of the region and regional corridors and connectivity projects. Besides the key findings here are some possible future scenarios, which could be viewed purely as a perception for future development. These are the following:

- Revival of Silk Route will increase the information flow.
- Cooperation in the labour movement will increase with the development of transport corridors.
- External powers will continue to pursue self-centered foreign policies and objectives creating tension within the region.

Recommendations

Recommendations are such that the regional security challenges need to be addressed jointly and the time frame for completing the regional transport and connectivity projects should be maintained and effective implementation should be given the priority.

Conclusion

Strategic assessment on the possibilities of the revival of Silk Route connectivity through initiation of the regional transport corridors has been attempted to be provided here. Transport Corridor projects will indeed contribute significantly in developing trade and transit among the regional countries. Regional transport networks will increase India's engagement with Turkmenistan. Transport corridor would provide a platform to improve cooperation as well as communication and reduce barriers to permit the economies of each country to grow independently and achieve objectives for the benefit of the country and the region as a whole.

Nonetheless, for making these projects a success the vision has to be unified to achieve the common goal. As per Ashgabat Declaration prepared in September 2015, Turkmenistan will continue to pursue active policies aimed at addressing the concerns and challenges for reviving the Silk Route and developing connectivity for sustainable growth. Active foreign and trade policies, marketing support and political will are essential for achieving progress in developing regional transport network. Hence, all the benefiting states have to strive to harmonize their strategies complimenting each other and working in coordination with each other for getting the best result.

References

Akiner Shirin, Ibrahimov Rovshan, Ariz Huseynov. 'Interregional cooperation in Eurasia: Transport and Logistic projects as an accelerator of Integration within and between the Black sea region, the South Caucasus and Central Asia". *Special double issue*, Vol. 9-10, September 2013. pp 64-65 and 66-68.

Boulnois, Luce. Silk Road: Monks, Warriors and Merchants. Odyssey Books: Hong Kong, 2005. p. 66.

Boyer, Alan Lee. Recreating the Silk Road: The Challenges of over-coming transaction costs. *China and Eurasia* Vol. IV, No. 4, Central Asia—Caucasus Institute and Silk Route Studies Programme, 2006. pp. 72-74.

Eliseeff, Vadim. "Approaches Old and New to the Silk Roads". The Silk Roads: Highways of Culture and Commerce. UNESCO: Paris, 1998. Reprinted Berghahn Books, 2009. pp. 1–2

Firdous, T. "India and Central Asia". M.A. Kaw and A.A. Banday, ed. Central Asia Introspection. Crown Press: Srinagar, 2006. pp. 321-322.

Foltz, Richard. Religions of the Silk Road, 2nd ed. Palgrave Macmillan: New York, 2010.

Gosset, David. "Xinjiang and the revival of Silk Route". Greater China, 2000.

Medvedkov, Maxim Y."Regionalism or Globalization". "Russian-Eurasian Renaissance? US Trade and Investment in Russia and Eurasia". Jan. H. Kalicki and Eugene K. lawson, ed. Woodrow Wilson center press: Washington DC. pp. 43-50.

Nuriyev, Elkhan."South Caucasus at the cross road: Conflict, Caspian oil and great power politics". LI: Berlin, 2007. pp. 94-97

Roy, M.S. "India's Interest in Central Asia". *Strategic Analysis*, Vol. 34, (12), March 2001. pp. 2273–2289.

Sikri, Rajeev. *Challenge and Strategy*. Sage: India, 2009.

Singh, Anita. "India's Relations with Russia and Central Asia". *International Affairs*, 71(1), January 1999. pp. 69-81

Culture, History and Philosophy

Cultural Heritage of Turkmenistan

Durdymyrat Kuleyev

In today's prosperous times favorable conditions are created for all-round cooperation between national culture of Turkmenistan and cultures of the world in Turkmenistan. The Esteemed President of Turkmenistan Gurbanguly Berdimuhamedov who pays great attention to the development of national culture in the country has said: "*Intellectual values, indigenous features, traditions and wisdom of the courageous Turkmen people, which have been perfected for centuries, are embodied in our national culture.*"

The Turkmen people have immense national cultural heritage reflecting their centuries-old history. Turkmen smiths, jewelers, potters, carpet weavers, builders, painters and sculptors have preserved the great national art which will be passed on for centuries to come from one generation to another preserving the national spirit and national values.

Cultural life has become more active, and magnificent buildings for new theatres, museums, libraries have been constructed all over the vast land of Turkmenistan in order to stimulate the workers so that they further strive towards fulfilling new achievements to enrich the national cultural system.

Turkmenistan is by right recognized as the fifth center of origination and development of the world civilization and home of highly developed spiritual and material culture, ancient agriculture, cattle-breeding and original crafts along with Mesopotamia, Egypt, China and India. Many historical antiquities, including stone, bronze and ceramic products, ancient anaphora and massive seals, stone and terracotta figurines, finely encrusted rhytons, jewels of filigree work, and also stylish ornaments on their surfaces, mainly of vegetation and geometric forms, which have been found during the archeological excavations, give a clear idea of centuries-old cultural progress.

Large states during the Middle-Ages, such as Merv, Nisa, Koneurgench, Amul, Abiverd, Dehistan were located along the largest trade routes of the Great Silk Road. The witnessing of rapid development of culture, crafts, art and science in these cities graphically demonstrates existence of dynamic cultural exchanges at that time. The interactions between Turkmen, Greek, Arabian, Persian and Indian cultures promoted mutually advantageous progress of civilizations.

At present, 7570 cultural sites are registered in Turkmenistan, 3945 or 52.1 percent of which are rated as archaeological heritage. Three largest historical and cultural monuments in Turkmenistan have found their place in the UNESCO[1] World Heritage List. They are the historical and cultural complex of Ancient Merv, the Ancient Kunyaurgench and the antique Fortress Nisa - the capital city of the once powerful Parthian Empire.

The art of carpet weaving by the Turkmen people is one of the fields of the traditional original craft that has turned into an integral part of the cultural heritage, making an invaluable contribution to the universal cultural treasury.

The carpet weaving history dates back to ancient times. As a matter of fact, it traces the history of origination of the nation and historical destinies of the Turkmen people and inseparably links their heroic past, their admirable present and bright future with their lives. For many centuries handmade woolen carpets were not only used for the decoration of magnificent palaces, but they were also the pride of people of Turkmenistan. Notable for high durability, unfading (owing

1. UNESCO – United Nations Educational Scientific and Cultural Organization.

to natural dyes) brightness of paints the Turkmen carpets gained international recognition. Most of these products (*chuval*, bag, *hurjun*, *ensi*, etc.) carry purely functional character and are used in everyday life of Turkmen people. A thematic composition of carpet styles are based on geometrical shapes (rectangles, squares, circles, ovals, semicircles), harmoniously combined with vegetation and zoomorphic droplets.

The Art of undaunted skilled carpet weavers of Turkmenistan is now recognized as a true national heritage. Their laborious work and inexhaustible inspiration have created giant carpets - the real miracle of carpet-making. The first carpet was woven in 1942.

The giant carpet "*Galkynysh*" which is extremely complicated in style and manufacturing technique was recognized as one of the symbols of the prosperous epoch of Turkmenistan. The carpet "*Altyn asyr*" that went into the Guinness Book of Records, the "President" and the unique octahedral giant carpet "*Altyn Yildyz*" were all made in 2009. "*Cialkynysh ovazy*" is the largest giant carpet 352.8 square meters in size, every square meter of which contains about 340 thousand knots. The largest handmade carpet in the world is now stored at the National Museum of Turkmen Carpet where it is possible to see it. The smallest (0.01 m ~) carpets are also stored here. A separate part of exhibits consists of canvases - portraits, landscapes and pictures of monuments.

There is also the thickest carpet there, every square meter of which contains 1 million 148 thousand knots. In total, the richest museum exposition includes 8 thousand unique exhibits.

The book of the Esteemed President of Turkmenistan Gurbanguly Berdimuhamedov "*A Living Legend*" devoted to the ancient craft and high art of Turkmen carpet weaving was published in 2011. The Holiday of Turkmen Carpet which is already celebrated for more than 20 years has been marked every year widely in Turkmenistan as an important occasion for acknowledgement of world recognition of Turkmen national carpet-making and respect for the skills of undaunted carpet weavers of Turkmenistan.

The centuries-old historical process of development and perfection has turned the ancient jeweler's craft of Turkmenistan into the highest art showing beauty and giving true aesthetic pleasure. At the earliest stages jewels were represented by elementary ornamentation articles and artifacts made of small sea and river cockleshells, bones, stones, metal and glass. Gradually, materials and jewel manufacturing techniques were improved. The jewelers - *zergars* started to use gold, silver, different semi-precious stones more often as raw materials and transformed their products into true masterpieces. For most part, these products were intended for women and were luxury goods.

Modern jewels are notable for filigree work, fine workmanship and high artistic features. A wide choice of products includes beautiful specimen of ladies' jewelry and a separate group of jewelry consisting of trappings - bridle, harness and saddles encrusted with ivory and precious stones.

The Akhalteke horses, which for their peerless beauty and grace were called as the "Horses of Paradise" or "Heavenly racers" in different historical sources are another fine example of the centuries-old Turkmen horse-breeding tradition.

In his fundamental work "*Akhalteke Racer — Our Pride and Glory*" the Esteemed President of Turkmenistan Gurbanguly Berdimuhamedov wrote: "*the Akhalteke racers, bred by nature of the ancient Turkmen land and special talent of assiduous people, by their purity has outclassed all other breeds of race horses, being able to lead and set the example of horse-breeding art in the world. The 'winged' Akhalteke horses are the pride of the Turkmen land*".

Turkmen national music dates back to the ancient times. The cultural monuments written in medieval period bristle with descriptions of colorful scenes and spectacular celebrations, a characteristic part of which were national melodies and cheerful songs about glorious victories of the heroes. The people remember well many cherished and beautiful legends about the origin of traditional musical instruments: *dutar*, *gargy-tuyduk*, *gyjak*.

It is impossible to imagine Turkmen national festivities without original dances, which in spirit combines vestiges of ancient religious beliefs with elements of folk choreography. The most spectacular national dance is *kushtdepdi* and the folk dance *chapak* and melodious tunes of *lale*.

The Turkmen theatrical art is based on the traditions of folklore. Folk *destans* are the gemstones of the national art heritage, which provide the richest material for the development of dramaturgy.

Cinematography is one of the fields of creative work. Many literary works are adapted as films. Turkmen people celebrate many holidays. The main holidays, which are widely marked as symbols of unity, friendship and brotherhood by the Turkmen people, are - "Independence Day of Turkmenistan", "Day of National Flag of Turkmenistan", "Neutrality Day", "Day of Revival, Unity and Poetry of Magtymguly Pyragy", and also such traditional national religious holidays, as "*Novruz*", "*Kurban Bairam*" and "*Oraza Bairam*". Besides that, there are such holidays, as "Day of Turkmen Racer", "*Galla Bairam*", "Day of Carpet", "A drop of water - a grain of gold", "Good Neighborliness", etc. The prosperous epoch of Turkmenistan symbolizes a new stage in preservation, restoration and popularization of the national cultural heritage.

Turkmenistan pays foremost attention to the active cultural relations with the neighboring states and supports partnership with the developed countries in the areas of culture and economy and sincerely wishes for consolidation of peace all over the world.

Sufism

The Mystic Path of Peace

Meeta Narain

Sufism is a mystical movement found all over the Islamic world, which has a deep influence on the different people of the Middle-East. It is well known that along the Silk Route, not only textiles and spices, but also religions were exchanged. Islam was the dominant religion among the Silk Route traders which brought with it, its belief, systems and a culture rich in tradition and advancements to the millions of people.

Amongst the expanding Muslim empire and Islamic beliefs, Sufism sprung-up as a cult in search for direct mystical knowledge of God and his love, its goal being 'to progress beyond mere intellectual knowledge to a mystical experience that submerged limited man in the infinity of God'[1]. Relevance of Sufism in today's world is very pertinent as a source of peace and neutrality to face the growing changes in the globalized world. It is interesting to study its expanse today and its existence in the regions of Silk Route—Turkmenistan being one of them. Since the year 2015 has been marked as the Year of Peace and Neutrality in Turkmenistan, the philosophy of Sufism amongst other beliefs plays a dynamic role in portraying the deep personal identities of people trying to adopt techniques developed to achieve the goal of a blissful union with the ultimate reality.

1. http://www.angelfire.com/az/rescon/SUFIMYSTIC.HTML

The neutrality of Turkmenistan, its policy of peace, good neighbourliness and development envelop Turkmenistan's approach towards respecting movements, which play a crucial role in dealing with issues of global importance—and hence the focus here is on this mystical movement—Sufism, its historical growth, its contribution and relevance in the global transformations and as a major source of providing neutrality and peace to the region of Turkmenistan and subsequently to the world. Three important aspects of this movement are studied here—the emergence, the growth and the relevance of Sufism today, in particular to Turkmenistan.

Emergence of Sufism

Sufism, a mystical form of Islam that has flourished in the Muslim world for centuries has enjoyed a strong revival in Central Asia. In the article, ***Sufism in Central Asia: A Force for Moderation or a Cause of Politicization?*** Martha Brill Olcott explores Sufism's potential to become a major movement, including political movement as well in Central Asia by analyzing the movement's history and current leaders in Central Asia, particularly in Uzbekistan and Turkmenistan[1].

Much has been written to explore the expanse of Sufism as a mass movement—the future role Sufism will play in Central Asia is dependent on both secular and religious circumstances. Olcott also states that a reasonable balance between Sufis and fundamentalists is a necessity. Since Sufism currently poses little threat to the secular ideology of Central Asian states, there is a need to understand the government policies towards supporting the Sufism ideology so as to maintain a balance between all the existing movements.[2]

All along the Silk Road for much of this time, Islam was the dominant religion among Silk Road traders coming from western Eurasia, and they brought with them a system rich in culture and

1. This is the third paper in an ongoing project for a forthcoming book on Islam and Central Asia by Martha Brill Olcott http://carnegieendowment.org/2007/06/06/sufism-in-central-asia-force-for-moderation-or-cause-of-politicization
2. *Ibid.*

tradition to the masses. Trade of textiles, spices and even religions that were exchanged along the Silk Road starting around 1,000 B.C. continued for several millennia. The religious beliefs of people along the Silk Road at the beginning of the 1st century BC were very different from what they would later become.[1] That the religious beliefs of the peoples of the Silk Road changed drastically from what they had been when trans-Eurasian trade began to take place on a regular basis was largely due to the effects of travel and trade on the Silk Road itself. Over the centuries for two thousand years the Silk Road remained a network of roads for the travel and dissemination of religious beliefs across Eurasia. Religious belief is often one of the most important and deeply held aspects of personal identity, and people are reluctant to go where they cannot practice their own faith. Traders who used the Silk Road regularly therefore built shrines and temples of their own faiths wherever they went, in order to maintain their own beliefs and practices of worship while they were far from home. Missionaries of many faiths accompanied caravans on the Silk Road, consciously trying to expand the reach of their own religious persuasion and make converts to their faith.[2]

The emergence of Sufism, as not an ethnic or religious group, but a mystical movement is found all over the Islamic world and still has a deep influence on the varied populations of the Middle East. Sufism grew historically as a reaction against the rigid legalism of the orthodox religious leadership and as a counterweight to the growing worldliness of the expanding Muslim empire.

One source of Sufism is to be found in the twofold presentation of God in the Qur'an: on the one hand he is described as the almighty creator, lord and judge, and on the other hand he is seen as abiding in the believer's heart and nearer to man than his own jugular vein. Sufism searches for a direct mystical knowledge of God and of His love. Its goal was to progress beyond mere intellectual knowledge to

---

1. Islam's Influence on the Silk Roads *by Taylor Echolls*, Demand Media http://people.opposingviews.com/islams-influence-silk-roads-5002.html
2. http://asiasociety.org/belief-systems-along-silk-roads

a mystical (existential) experience that submerged limited man into the infinity of God. It used Jewish, Christian, Gnostic, Hellenistic, Zoroastrian and Hindu traditions that were brought into Islam by converts from the many conquered populations.

Sufism had an important part in the formation of Muslim societies as it educated the masses and met their felt needs, giving spiritual meaning to their lives and channeling their emotions. Sufis were also great missionaries who converted new regions to Islam. Its cultural contribution was a rich poetry in Arabic, Persian, Turkish, Urdu, Sindhi, Pashto and Punjabi, which spread its mystical ideas all over the Muslim world and enriched local literature and identity.

Several techniques were developed to achieve the goal of a blissful union with the Ultimate Reality. They were known as *Dhikr* (remembrance, mention of God) and *Sama*' (hearing). In the *Dhikr* Sufis would recite the many names of God and sing hymns of praise. Special forms of breathing were supposed to aid concentration and help them attain an ecstatic state in which they actually felt they had reached union with God. During the *Sama*', poetry, music and dance were used as an aid to reaching the ecstatic state.

These informal groups later crystallized into Sufi brotherhoods gathered around famous leaders. In some countries even today most Muslims belong to one order or another. Around the Muslim world there are hundreds of orders and they are an important religious and political force. Sufism is found amongst both Sunnis and Shi'a, being a movement within the orthodox Islam. However it has many links with Isma'ilism and other extreme Shi'a sects (*Ghulat*) as it developed in similar times and circumstances.

Muhammad is regarded as the first Sufi master who passed his esoteric teachings orally to his successors who also received his special grace (*barakah*). An unbroken chain of transmission of divine authority is supposed to exist from Muhammad to his successor 'Ali and from him down to generations of Sufi masters (*Sheikhs*, *Pirs*). Each order has its own *Silsilah* (chain) that links it with Muhammad and 'Ali.[1]

---

1. http://www.angelfire.com/az/rescon/SUFIMYSTIC.HTML

Growth of Sufism

Over a period of centuries, Islam in Turkmenistan has become an unusual blend of Sufi mysticism, orthodox (Sunni) Islam, and shamanistic and Zoroastrian practices. The cult of ancestors is still observed, and reverence for members of the four holy tribes (the *owlat*) is still strong. Popular or 'folk' Islam is centered on practices and beliefs related to Sufism, the mystical dimension of Islam that originated in Central Asia. The veneration of holy places, which are generally tombs connected with Sufi saints, mythical personages, or tribal ancestors, continues to play an active role in the preservation of religious feeling among the population.[1]

The pervasive nature of folk Islam, together with the Soviet-era repression of religion and the authoritarian nature of the country's political system, have acted as barriers to the growth of Islamist ideology in Turkmenistan. Thus, the leadership has sought to capitalize on the popularity of Sufism in order to encourage religion to conform to local popular practices as well as to combat the emergence of Islamism. As in other parts of Central Asia, the distinction between religious and 'national' rituals is blurred in Turkmenistan; since the perestroika period of the late 1980s, the leadership has attempted to co-opt Islam as a fundamental component of its overarching nation-building campaign.[2]

In much of Central Asia, the broad process of re-Islamization that took place in the late 1980s and early 1990s was accompanied by the emergence of political movements that espoused a greater adherence to Islamic tenets. In Turkmenistan, however, there has been no movement to introduce elements of *Sharia* or to establish parties based on Islamic principles. The vast majority of the population appears to prefer to disassociate religion from politics altogether, and would unlikely be lending support to any attempt to replace secular with religious rule, especially if it were to involve a political struggle.

1. http://almanac.afpc.org/Turkmenistan#
2. *Ibid.*

Like in other Central Asian republics in the post-Soviet period, in Turkmenistan also political authorities have sought to curb Islamist trends by promoting a vision of Islam, intimately connected to Sufism, that is concerned with the preservation of national traditions and combating extremism. Similar to neighboring republics the government here too has allowed Sufi practices, such as the veneration of local saints and local shrine visitation, to flourish, and they have successfully contained any potential criticism of these practices by those who subscribe to more fundamental forms of ideology.

To explain this fact and to quote from the works of Emily O'Dell of Columbia University Western scholars and politicians have recently suggested that Sufism should be encouraged in Central Asia to combat extremist ideologies, especially in republics of Uzbekistan, Tajikistan and Turkmenistan, which have been implementing this approach for many years by investing money in preserving centuries-old shrines of Sufi saints, publishing ancient Sufi manuscripts, and promoting Sufism in Islamic education. The transformative spiritual and political power of Sufism in the contemporary Muslim world, especially in Central Asia, cannot be underestimated or ignored, and governments in Central Asia are well aware of its potential to both advance the goals of the national project and to act as an underground vehicle of resistance to the national Islam and politics promoted by the state.[1]

As in other Central Asian states, Turkmenistan authorities have sought to limit unwanted Islamist trends by promoting a vision of Islam that is concerned with the preservation of tradition. In similar fashion to neighboring Uzbekistan, the leadership has attempted to capitalize on the popularity of Sufism in order to encourage religion to conform to local popular practices as well as to combat the emergence of Islamism.

Consequently, Turkmenistan's leadership has taken some steps to foster the Sufi tradition and incorporate it into the regime's larger

1. The Teaching, Practice, And Political Role Sufism In Dushanbe - Emily O'Dell, Columbia University, 2011 - http://www.ucis.pitt.edu/nceeer/2011_825-01h_O%27Dell.pdf

nation-building project. Thus, the Niyazov leadership provided the mosque and mausoleum complex of the twelfth-century Sufi scholar, Hoja Yusup Hamadani, with a modern-day reconstruction. Located in the Mary Region, this holy site is one of the most important places of shrine pilgrimage in Turkmenistan, remaining open even during the Soviet period, albeit under strict control. Likewise, rather than seeking to prohibit local pilgrimages to sacred places, both the Niyazov and Berdimuhammedov governments have encouraged it, even providing free accommodation for pilgrims in some instances. In 2009, citing fears concerning the spread of swine flu, Turkmenistan's authorities barred aspiring Muslim pilgrims from making the hajj to Saudi Arabia altogether, urging them instead to sojourn to 38 sacred sites across the country, although most of the sites had historical or cultural rather than religious significance. As of 2013, the Turkmenistan's government has shown no signs of easing pressure on Muslims, with censorship, educational and legal restrictions remaining tightly in place.[1]

Relevance of Sufism

Sufism has been integral in defining the cultural, political, behavioural and economic interaction of Central Asians since its arrival in the seventh century. Hence, its resurgence is neither surprising nor unintelligible. Despite bans on unofficial religious activity, Sufism received widespread allegiance at the grassroots level during the Soviet period.

Sufis help the people irrespective of caste, creed, religion, faith, belief and sex. They are broadminded people having universal vision. They follow the path of Islam, founded on divine love, universal charity and human compassion which also enshrine righteousness, piousness, truthfulness and kindness.

The word *Sufism,* popularly known as mysticism is most likely derived from the Arabic word *suf* (meaning "wool"), more specifically,

1. http://almanac.afpc.org/Turkmenistan#

it mean "the person wearing ascetic woolen garments". Sufism is deeply rooted within Islam and its development began in the late 7th and 8th centuries. The Sufis love their creator, cherish the desire of His closeness and follow His path. According to Islam, there are two types of service. Throughout the night, they remain in prayer, meditation and contemplation of Allah and throughout the day, they serve His creatures, especially human beings.

The vast regions which stretch from India (especially Northern India), to Iran, Afghanistan, Central Asia, and Anatolia (Turkey) had close interaction throughout history. The people of these regions with different ethnic backgrounds, cultures and languages have been intermingling for many centuries, as seen in the cross-current exchanges of religious ideas and beliefs.[1]

The mystic movement of Sufism contains elements of New Platonism, Judaism, Christianity, Zoroastrianism, and particularly of Buddhism. In essence, Sufism propagates asceticism, pantheism, and mysticism. As such Sufism is totally unique to Islam and remains an important strand as a calming influence even in the context of violence and terrorism in the name of Islam. Their impact on many parts of the world is so deeply rooted that it forms a significant part of popular religious beliefs and practices till today.

---

1. Concept note by Dr. Nazir Raza Khan, Asst. Professor Academy of International Studies, Jamia Milia Islamia, New Delhi http://www.scribd.com/doc/248807668/Conference-Ais-2015february11-12#scribd

Message of Brotherhood and Fellow Feeling in Magtymguly's Poetry

Akhtarul Wasey

Magtymguly Pyragy is widely believed to have been born in the Hajygowshan village near Gonbad-e-Qabus city in what is now the Iranian province of Golestan, the northern steppes of which are known as Turkmen Sahra ("Turkmen steppes"). In his poetry, Magtymguly Pyragy says "*Tell those who enquire about me that I am a Gerkez, I hail from Etrek and my name is Magtymguly*", identifying his homeland as the banks of the Etrek River and expressing his identity through his tribe.

He received his early education in Persian and Arabic languages from his father Döwletmämmet Azady, a leading scholar at that time. He went on to study at various madrasahs, including the Idris Baba Madrasah in the village of Gyzyl Ayak, the Madrasah of Shir Gazi Khan in Khiva, and may have also studied in Bukhara for some time.[1] Upon his return home, Magtymguly Pyragy worked as a silversmith while he taught and wrote.[2] He went on to develop a realistic style of writing of the 18th century Turkmen language that proved very popular and ultimately led to him becoming one of the most cherished

1. Youssef Azemoun, trans, "An Interview with Gara Ishan", *Journal of Makhtumkuli Studies*, 2(2000).
2. *Ibid.*

Turkmen poets of all times. He was also a devout Naqshbandi Sufi who was said to have traveled through all the lands comprising modern Turkmenistan, teaching and praying for the salvation of his people. There are various views, concerning the poetic world of Magtymguly Pyragy, and his scientific biography. It is connected with preservation and non-preservation of historical data about the life of the poet as well as a part of his literary heritage uptill now. It gave rise to various views regarding the year of his birth and death as well as family life of Magtymguly. In the biography of Magtymguly Pyragy the years of his birth and death were defined as 1733 and 1782. These years of the poet's birth and death are chosen in his biography on the basis of the book "*Traveling to Central Asia*" by A.Vambery. In his book A. Vambery wrote: "*He (Magtymguly-A.A.) is from Gokleng tribe of the Turkmen people.*"[1]

He promoted the idea of keeping the Turkmen way sacred, as well as maintaining the unity and integrity of the Turkmen nation. During his lifetime, his efforts of overcoming the existing tribal loyalties and rivalries had minimal success. The Turkmen tribes of the 18th century were torn by internecine strifes and the aggressions of powerful neighbors. Much of Magtymguly Pyragy's poetry depicts the suffering of the common people caused by the selfish predations of those in power. He also criticized rulers and many religious figures for their exploitation of the poor and their mockery of justice in such stanzas as: "*Khans of Gokleng have been spoiled/They think we do not deserve any comfort/They took away all our belongings/ We could not do anything but watch them,*" and "*Rulers dispense no justice anymore/Muftis issue justice for a farthing*".[2]

The simple yet profound quality of his poems has, over two centuries, dominated the minds of not only the Turkmens, but all Turkic peoples living in the vast region from the Oxus to the Transcaucasia. Berdak, a Karakalpak classical poet said: "*I worship*

1. Армени Вамбери, Путешествие по Средней Азии, Спб. 1865, стр.. 159.
2. Youssef Azemoun, trans, "An Interview with Gara Ishan", *Journal of Makhtumkuli Studies*, 2(2000).

Magtymguly's every word". Vambery wrote that the poems of Magtymguly Pyragy were second to the Koran among the Turkmen people.

For many Magtymguly Pyragy is so revered that he is something more than a poet - a saint perhaps. He is a poet of the highest spiritual order. He has written on a variety of themes - mystical, lyrical, religious, social, patriotic and others which make his poems appeal to various strata among the Turkmens and other people. This quality made Magtymguly Pyragy a national poet even when he was alive. V. V. Bartold, a distinguished Russian Orientalist, wrote: "*Magtymguly, who is a Gokleng, is the national poet of the Turkmens; including the Turkmens of Stavropol......*[1] *The only people among the Turkic peoples who have a national poet are the Turkmens*".[2] Magtymguly Pyragy exerted an enormous influence on the development of Turkmenian poetry. His poetry is organically connected with folk poetry.

Magtymguly altered the Turkmenian poetic language, bringing it closer to the popular speech and replacing the *aruz* with the popular syllabic system.

Magtymguly Pyragy suffered for the fate of his people. He saw their basic misfortune - the impossibility of getting rid of the knout of the enslavers as a consequence of the non-cohesion of the Turkmen tribes. His thoughts about the national liberation of the Turkmens are unclear but he felt clearly that the national unity of the Turkmen tribes was impossible given the mercenariness of their feudal ruling clique. That is why he was against the representatives of that clique. It was precisely he, Magtymguly Pyragy, the poet and thinker, who thereby defined the democratic direction of the entire later struggle of the best representatives of the Turkmen people for the unity of Turkmen tribes, for their liberation from the yoke of alien enslavers. And herein lays his greatness and his enormous service.

Magtymguly Pyragy's poetical-philosophical literary heritage remains at the bottom of the heart of the nation as a love-saga to

1. Sochineniya, Vol. 2, p. 614, 1963.
2. *Ibid.* Vol. 5, p. 187, 1968.

Almighty, Homeland, human being, nature and life. Magtymguly's literary heritage is highly appreciated not only for the richness of its language or beauty and diversity of its style, but also for the development of wise philosophical thoughts, for the masterful depiction of the different sides of secular life, and for the contribution to the human intelligence. Magtymguly Pyragy paved the way to the human soul by using the perfect methods of thinking, consolidating his philosophical thoughts with good feelings about the world, humanity, motherland, love and remains forever in the memory of the people.

Magtymguly Pyragy, first of all, is the national poet of Turkmen people, at the same time he is thinker-humanist who cared about all human beings, and his care for others has been revealed through his love for the Turkmen people. His love for creativity, peaceful life in the country and his rebellious thinking to improve the fate of the ordinary people made him prominent and took him outside the national boundaries. A personality who serves faithfully to mankind can be useful for everyone; a person who won the hearts of his people can win souls of others as well. The poet expressed his philosophical views through poetical precepts that a man should strive for spiritual perfection. He appealed to his contemporaries to build a fearless society because he knew the essence of freedom and the motive of the conflicts; he called upon his people to understand the human nature, be sensible, unite and create a statehood. Great poet left us an enormous heritage of poetic treasure which is full of wisdom and sweet feelings and wish for peace and prosperity for his people whom he wanted to see educated and successful. Healthy judgment of his verses serves as an admirable guideline not only for the Turkmen people but also for the spiritual needs of humanity. It is the poetic world of this lyricist that became gem for human knowledge. At present people of different countries and cultures can read and enjoy the beauty of his verses, which makes one think about life and social problems. His fine verses became songs for beloved and his wisdom serves as proverbs and sayings for ordinary and educated; for this reason they are translated into many languages of the world.

Magtymguly Pyragy is the healer of human soul. Many centuries have passed since he wrote his poetry, but as the time goes by the value of his verses increases, because his precepts and admonitions have the impact like that of healing of the wounds and they inspire souls. By reading Magtymguly Pyragy, depressed people feel relief and comfort; weak ones gain strength and power. Turkmen people addressed him at the times of hardships and also in the times of big conflicts and war and they found way out of their problems. His words encouraged young and old at different times in history and contributed to the spiritual revival of the Turkmen society. It is true that his poetry is pure like mountain spring and fresh like morning breeze, beautiful like field of tulips, fragrant like grassland flowers and sweet like melody of *dutar*. In general, Magtymguly Pyragy's poetry is a spiritual balm for the soul.

Magtymguly Pyragy lived in the historical period when there were many wars and conflicts between countries and he was deeply affected by those hardships and difficulties. Personal and social sufferings shaped him to be a sensible philosopher and knowledgeable scholar of his time. He studied the religious and secular sciences of his time and cognized the world; he differentiated evil and good and passed all stages of spiritual perfection and became the perfect human. Uniqueness of Magtymguly Pyragy is that he appealed to each and every disintegrated Turkmen tribe of that time to unite and consolidate as a nation and create a state. He is considered "Great" because he was the first poet to consider all Turkmens as one nation and was the advocator of his ideas. The wisdom of Magtymguly Pyragy is that he criticized unfriendliness and disagreement and fought for the union of the Turkmen people. At present Turkmen people educate their children and young with help of the lessons taught by Magtymguly Pyragy and time proved that his ideas about a powerful state were true.

Magtymguly Pyragy was a Sufi. He sought the blessing of a Sufi leader. A Sufi by the name of Shah Glirbat, was told that a poet who was a Turkmen wished to see him. He said he did not want to see a poet who spoke nonsense. Magtymguly Pyragy then wrote his famous poem "*I Took Up My Pen*" which gives an insight into his enormous literary learning. He compared the Sufi to "a young hawk with feathers still not grown." According to a story the Sufi travelled a long way to meet Magtymguly Pyragy and apologized.

Magtymguly Pyragy attached great importance to the Truth and the concept of a perfect man, as a Sufi would do. However, the human suffering and social injustice which he witnessed around himself made him pay attention to worldly matters too. He became more interested in the concept of the happiness of his people. Even in his mystic poem like "The Riddle: A Vision" he defends justice, moral values and the oppressed. Viewing life from the point of view of human morality became a part and parcel of the sense of humanity and his love for people. It was these feelings that made it impossible for him to come to terms with the corruption and injustice in the society. In the following lines he depicts the position of the poor:

The poor man, goes barefoot, showing his need,
At meetings they will seat him low indeed,
While if he rides a horse it's called an ass –
A rich man's ass of course, is called a steed!

He cannot do much to help the poor, who are despised even by their own close relatives, but encourages them that even if it might be the Judgement Day - they should be strong:

Oppressors then it'll have to play the moke –
The poor; of course will be the bravest lion.

He harshly criticizes the oppressor and corrupt people of society:

Sultans now laugh at justice in eclipse.
These derelictions all spell apocalypse.
When far'hi-igs buy a miftis best decree.
And tyrants die with no prayer in their lips.

Conclusion

Magtymguly Pyragy is revered by the Turkmens in general, irrespective of their tribal differences. Information concerning the life of this national poet is quite limited. It is known that he was of the Gokleng tribe, was of great erudition, and according to his own words, was blessed with a vision - in a dream he saw Omar, from whom he received the gift of poetic invention. The story of this vision is the opening piece in manuscripts of Magtymguly Pyragy's works, and there is hardly a Turkmen who does not know this song by heart.

Being of Gokleng in origin, Magtymguly Pyragy constantly dreamt of an end to the age-old enmity between his tribe and another Turkmen tribe, the Yomud, and of forming a close-knit union against the common foe, Persia. The Turkmen people have no doubt that Magtymguly Pyragy was a holy man; everything that he wrote or said will come true sooner or later, say the Turkmen. Thus, the Turkmen people explained their last uprising against the Persians in 1867 and the appearance of a certain Afghan, Sultan Mahmed Khan, who became leader of the rebels, by a prediction made by Magtymguly Pyragy, but the last part of the prediction—which said that Astrabad would be captured and the whole of Persia subjugated by the Turkmen—was not destined to come true.

Revisiting the Principle of Neutrality and Peace through the Discourse of Magtymguly Pyragy

Naseem Ahmad Shah

It is very hard to find any nation across the world that does not experience the effects of political, economic, social or religious polarization. But Turkmenistan is one such nation that, in addition to its Sovereign and independent character preferred, twenty years ago on December 12, 1995, the path of neutrality and non-alignment. The commitment of Turkmen nation and state towards its neutral character could not be influenced even by such political and economic developments that changed the whole scenario of geopolitical relations in the contemporary world. The foreign policy and diplomacy adopted by Turkmenistan continues to attest and corroborate its commitment towards non-alignment and demonstrates a manifestation of high ideals like co-existence, tolerance and peace.

This book of articles reminds everyone of the historic cultural, linguistic, ethnic and economic ties between India and Turkmenistan - the two sovereign and independent nations of the Silk Route region. India being the pioneer of the concept of non-alignment and neutrality has all along offered its support and cooperation to Turkmenistan in strengthening its position both at the regional as well as the international level.

Among all Central Asia nations Turkmenistan enjoys a special position as a neutral neighbour. This is proved by the continuous increase in the bilateral relations, diplomatic engagements, trade adventures and cultural exchanges between the two countries. During the recent years a lot of steps have been taken by Turkmenistan to revive and revisit the cultural cooperation between the two nations particularly in the field of literature and culture. Various Indian specialists and scientists were invited to international scientific conferences that were held in Turkmenistan to highlight the mutual impact and interaction between the two nations in the field of literary and cultural discourse.

To appreciate the passion of Indian scholars for revitalizing Indo-Turkmen literary and cultural ties, in June 2014 a delegation was invited to Ashkabad to participate in the Jubilee celebrations of Magtymguly Pyragy. As a pioneer and as an advocate of freedom, sovereignty, justice and brotherhood he has rightly been called a symbol of Turkmen nationhood.

The literature of Turkmen language represents one of the landmarks of their cultural and civilization history. The literary legacy of Turkmen language is highly colourful and complex in nature. Their literature in general and the genre of poetry in particular embodies the essence of the Turkmen literary discourse during the 18th century displaying its fullest range in the intimacy, intensity and precision in the poems of Magtymguly Pyragy (1733-82), whom the Turkmen see as one of the founders of their literature. According to Barthold "*the only people among the Turkic peoples who have a national poet are the Turkmen.*"

Turkmen literature assumed its full identity after the emergence of Magtymguly Pyragy in the 18th century. The simple yet profound quality of his poems has, over two centuries, dominated the minds of not only the Turkmen, but all Turkic people living in the vast region from the Oxus to the Transcaucasia.

Magtymguly Pyragy's poetry represents many aspects of social change, behaviour patterns, hopes, repressed wishes, creative thoughts, subconscious yearnings and collective dreams. It analyses the social ethos in the geographical frame with reference to its beauty, emotions, dreams, miseries, diversity and complexity of interpretation. This made him a national poet even during his own time.

As a representative of Turkmen poetry, Magtymguly Pyragy's reputation rests both on his discursive as well as the lyric tradition that exist in his poems. At best he surpasses perhaps most of his contemporaries in length and breadth of his imagination, the forcible rhythm of his words, depth of emotions and tenderness of feelings. His poetic discourses in general and his patriotic songs in particular gave the Turkmen nation a great monument of patriotic thought. Following the tradition of Magtymguly Pyragy the discourse of patriotism itself became a convention to be followed by a host of poets in Central Asia, Persia, India and Turkey. His inclusion of street wisdom in classical forms and his simplicity of language contributed to his popularity with travelling bards. With regard to politics, he developed the concepts of state and individuality. He thought that when people focus on self-preservation, they head towards a catastrophe of destroying each other. According to him, the state and its rulers were created with the sole purpose of avoiding such a catastrophe, preventing fights between the people and securing peace in the country. He had only one cherished slogan for Turkmen nation "*a nation ruled by wise men where friendship and fairness govern*". At the end of his life, all his works were confiscated by the Persians. Magtymguly Pyragy personally witnessed how the camel on which his manuscripts were loaded fell into a river and was swept away.

There are over a hundred manuscripts of Magtymguly Pyragy's collected poems in Turkmenistan, and many others in Iran, Afghanistan and other places; there is one manuscript of Magtymguly Pyragy's poems at the British Library which also has poems by other Turkmen classical poets.

Magtymguly Pyragy was introduced to the Western literary world last to last century after the translation of three of his 'songs' into English by Alexander Chodzko in 1842 in London, and the publication of thirty poems in Turkmen with German translations by the Hungarian scholar Vambery, who carried out research into the poet's life during his excursion to Central Asia last century. However, during the recent years Magtymguly Pyragy's poetry has been translated into a number of languages including French, Arabic and Urdu as well.

The exact date and place of Magtymguly Pyragy's birth is not known. He is believed to have been born in 1733. He was the third son of Dowletmamet Azadi, who is also known as Garry Molla (1700-1765). Azadi was a great poet, a writer, scholar and author of several books. Magtymguly was named after his grandfather, Magtymguly Yonarchy (1654-1720). He belonged to the Gyshyklar clan of the Gerkez division of the Gokleng tribe of the Turkmens. Magtymguly Pyragy's father was his first teacher and mentor. His father sent the young Magtymguly to a teacher called Niyaz Salih. During his studies Magtymguly Pyragy also acquired the skills of a silversmith and a saddler. He studied in a Madrasah called Idris Baba; he continued his education in Bukhara and finished it at the Shir Gaza Madrasah in Khiva where his talent was recognized and he was appointed a "*khalifa*", a substitute teacher. He mastered classical Arabic, Persian and Turkic languages and literature, beside his religious education. He returned home and began teaching at his village while continuing the craft of a silversmith.

For Magtymguly Pyragy the Truth was of great importance. He, as a Sufi, had the idea of a perfect man. However, the suffering and injustice that he saw around him drew his attention to worldly matters as well. He wanted his people to be happy. In his mystic poem like "*The Riddle: A Vision*" he defends the oppressed.

He suffered a tragic personal and family life amid endemic tribal conflicts which intensified in the 18th century as the Turkmens became fragmented into smaller groups. This made it easy for the neighbouring rulers and khans to invade and plunder Turkmen territory. It was during such an invasion that Magtymguly Pyragy lost the fruit of years of hard and devoted work when the contents of his house, including his manuscripts, were taken away on camels. It is said that Magtymguly saw the camel carrying his manuscripts slip, hurling the manuscripts into the river Etrek, thus making the river an enemy of the poet.

The poem *"Making My Dear Life Lost"* recounts this sad event:

Making my dear life lost to all that's good,
An evil fate wrought awesome sacrilege,
Hurling the books I'd written to the flood,
To leave me bookless with my grief and rage.

Magtymguly Pyragy was a man concerned with the welfare of his people. There are tales which say that he personally resolved disputes between various tribes. He believed that the whole tragedy of the Turkmens was due to the quarrels and disunity among the tribes. In some of his poems he warns his people against internecine strife. Having realized the dangers of tribalism, he in his poem "*Exhortation in the Time of Trouble*", calls upon the Turkmen tribes, calling them by their names to unite into a single national state, thus becoming the first Turkmen poet to introduce such a political theme into Turkmen literature. He says:

If Turkmens would only tighten the Belt of Determination
They could drink the Red Sea in their strength,
So let the tribes of Teke, Yomut, Goklen, Yazir, and Alili
Unite into one proud nation.

According to widespread stories, Magtymguly Pyragy died as a result of the unbearable grief due to sad experiences in his old age, aggravated by his distress at the tribal hostility which had caused him so much suffering. The date of his death is not known, but it is thought to be towards the end of the 18th century or the beginning of the 19th century. Before his death he sat at his open door to look for the last time at the splendour of the mountains which had been so much a part of his life. Here is how the poem "*When I Cease to Be*" ends:

Whoever lives will soon in graves have lain;
Says Makhtumkuli, death devours all sins.
The sky remains, while earth in orbit spins,
The sun will rise and set, moon wax and wane.

He wrote some poems in the classical forms, but most of them use the popular form "*qoshuk*". Qoshuks are poems consisting of quatrains with lines of eight or eleven (or occasionally seven) syllables. This form of poem, lucidly written and rooted in folklore, creates a musicality which suits Turkmen folk music and makes it easily understood and eagerly taken up by "*Bashkhis*", the folk singers. This is one of the reasons why his poems have spread over a vast area from Central Asia to the Caucasus. His *qoshuks* generally have the rhyming scheme of A, B, C, B in the first stanza and C, C, C, B and D, D, D, B and so on in the remaining stanzas.

As the first poet to introduce political themes, social criticism and even new forms into Turkmen literature, Magtymguly Pyragy wrote on an enormous variety of subjects which appeal to various strata of Turkmen and other Turkic people. For this reason some see him as a spiritual leader and a teacher, others as a patriot and a guide leading his people to happiness. To the Turkmen he is "Magtymguly Bagtyng guly"—the Bestower of Happiness.

The historic character of the creativity of Magtymguly Pyragy is a distinctive feature of the Turkmen and Turkic language speaking poets, who created their works of literature earlier than him. The poet depicts the definite historical events in his works that took place on the Turkmen land, he takes hard the death of his contemporaries, who perished for peaceful life of the Turkmen people, and the joy of people gladdened and inspired him. Perhaps, we do not meet lines similar to the following ones, written by Magtymguly Pyragy, in the creativity of the Turkic speaking poets, who wrote their works of literature before him:

Magtymguly, it is an ill fate,
Troubles me much,

The Turkmen people, the whole nation,
I see them on peaceful land.

One can feel the mastery of a great personality in them. Magtymguly Pyragy connected literature with the life of people. The lives of people of the 18th century have found its embodiment in poems by him. One can read in Magtymguly Pyragy's verses about the historical and political events that took place in the lives of Turkmen people in the 18th century, the traditions and customs of the Turkmen people, the character features peculiar to the Turkmen women and girls as well as the whole Turkmen people in general. But the character of the poet's works is not the same in various periods of his creativity.

The themes of Fatherland, peaceful life, unity of people, statehood are the well-elaborated ones in the discourse of Magtymguly Pyragy. He considered all these themes not separate from each other but as a single one connecting them with each other.

While speaking about Magtymguly Pyragy, one mainly talks about an ordinary human being, at least, an ordinary poet, but one should understand that he was not an ordinary person, that he had a great talent and unique spiritual world. If one does not do so, one will not be able to understand the natural gift of the outstanding personality who changed the Turkic literature completely and connected it with people's lives.

Rituals and Traditions of India and Turkmenistan

A Descriptive Study (Birth, Wedding and Death Ceremonies)

Mona Agnihotri

"Life is a ritual of love
Life is a ritual of union, and
Life is a dance of the divine"[1]
—Vishwas Chavan,
SoulBliss: a poetic tale of cosmic love

Introduction

The word '**Ritual**' is defined as—*"a formal ceremony or series of acts that are always performed in the same way."* The same dictionary defines the word '**Tradition**' as—*"a way of thinking, behaving, or doing something that has been used by the people in a particular group, family, society, etc. for a long time."*[2]

If one looks closely, the words ritual and tradition have similar differences as the words practice and theory–ritual being the practice

1. Vishwas Chavan, SoulBliss: A Poetic Tale of Cosmic Love, GoodReads, n.d., 5 February 2015, http://www.goodreads.com/quotes/tag/ritual
2. Merriam – Webster Dictionary, n.d., 5 February 2015, http://www.merriam-webster.com/dictionary/ritual

and tradition being the theory. Ritual is more objective and tradition is more subjective. But they are two sides of the same coin!

Every country, every culture, every subculture even has its own rituals and traditions. These rituals and traditions have been passed on from generation to generation and they work as guidelines for the society to carry on. Since any given culture has innumerable rituals and traditions, it becomes a huge task to study all of them together. Hence, this article attempts to study rituals and traditions of two ancient cultures/countries of Silk Road region—India and Turkmenistan, concentrating on the major ceremonial events of human life—birth, wedding and death.

Two Countries—Two Cultures

Since India and Turkmenistan are both ancient civilizations, their cultures are very rich with customs and traditions that are being followed for centuries and that have gone into making their folklore rich. Turkmen people love to sing songs for every occasion just like Indians do. There are songs for birth, for marriage, for death as well. Turkmen people even have songs for some of their social activities like carpet-weaving or camel milking.

There are a special group of people that are famous for their songs in Turkmenistan. They are called *bagshy/bakhshi*. This word is very interesting for the fact that in India there is a surname that resembles this word; this surname is *Bakshi*. It is believed that the Indian surname Bakshi originated from Persian which means Paymaster.[1] It was a title of an official whose duty was to distribute salaries in the army.

Bakhshis of Turkmenistan wander around towns and perform their songs in public. They sit on a carpeted pedestal and sing, sometimes from evening till the next morning and these performances attract a lot of public, sometimes in thousands! People gather around

1. Name Lab, n.d., Family Education, 7 February 2015, http://genealogy.familyeducation.com/surname-origin/bakshi

to listen to the bakhshis sing. This is very similar to a tradition that is popular in the Indian state of West Bengal in which a group of folk-singers called *bauls* perform their songs from evening till dawn and people gather around them to listen to them sing. Baul tradition is very popular in Bangladesh as well and it is an integral part of Bengali culture.

Another thing that is common in these two types of folk singing is the musical instruments that they use. There are some special musical instruments that the bakhshis play along with their vocal performances, one of which is called a *Dutar.*[1] Bauls of Bengal also carry a similar sounding musical instrument along with them called *Ektar/Ektara.* Both these musical instruments are stringed instruments. *Dutar* means two strings (from Iranian word *Du* which means two and *Tar* means string)[2] and *Ektar* means one string (from the word *Ek* which means one and *Tar* which means string). There is a bass-version of *Ektara* as well in India, which is called *Dotar/ Dotara* which sounds and looks very similar to Turkmen *Dutar*!

Singing of songs is an ancient tradition in India as well as in Turkmenistan. Both these countries have a rich collection of folksongs. These songs that are performed are taken from their legends, fairytales, folktales, poetry etc. In Turkmenistan these songs are called *destans.* As per the Internet newspaper Turkmenistan.ru—"*...destans are closely linked to the life of people depicting their centuries-old history, moral and domestic foundations.*"[3]

This word is also very similar in sound and meaning to the Urdu word *dastan* that is used in India and a few other Asian countries to denote a lyrical tale.

1. Folklore Traditions in Turkmenistan, n.d., Advantour, 8 February 2015, http://www.advantour.com/turkmenistan/culture/folklore.htm
2. *Ibid.*
3. Ancient folk destan "Sayatly Hemra" published for the first time in Turkmenistan, 24.03.06, Turkmenistan.ru, 8 February 2015, http://www.turkmenistan.ru/?page_id=3&lang_id=en&elem_id=7908&type=event&sort=date_desc

Some Common Rituals and Traditions in India and Turkmenistan

Human life is one big celebration right from his birth to his death. As Magtymguly Pyragy, the 18th century Turkmen poet once wrote—"*This world is full of noise; beginning with the celebration of a new born child and ending with weeping at his death.*"[1]

India and Turkmenistan are both ancient cultures and hence the rituals and traditions of these countries are deeply-rooted in day to day lives of their people. These rituals and traditions have become an integral part of their lives. Among all the traditions and customs, the most important for both the countries are those traditions that are connected to family life and relationships, like birth of a child, marriage ceremony or death of a loved one.

In both the countries, out of these three ceremonies, probably the most important and elaborate ceremony is that of a marriage. In India as well as Turkmenistan, people attach great importance to marriage. In both these countries marriage ceremony is not just a one day ceremony that takes place on the day of the wedding; it begins from the day the parents start looking for a match for their child. The match-making process is very important for both the cultures, as it is especially of utmost importance to find a suitable bride for the son. Attention is paid not only to the would-be bride and her qualities that would make the bride a good home maker, but also to her family and her background. Western concept of dating is not very common in India as well as Turkmenistan and marriages are mostly arranged. And even if a marriage is not arranged, the blessings of the parents are required in all the marriages.

In Turkmenistan parents consult the elders known as *aksakals* as well before finalizing a match. An auspicious day is even picked out for beginning of match-making and there are certain days that are

1. Gurbanjemal Iliyasova, and Amangul Karrieva, Turkmen Wedding Rites, Popular Beliefs, and Wedding Songs, n.d., 7 February 2015, http://www.turkmenhost.com/documents/Journal2/wedding.html

considered to bring success and good luck when something new is started on these days. "*The day of the wedding ceremony is fixed according to the advice of the aksakals, who ascertain the most favourable date, according to the location of certain stars and planets, and by the relation of the moon to the earth. The direction from which the bride arrives to the groom's home is also determined by the position of the stars. One particular star is considered very unlucky, and it is preferable to delay the wedding rather than have this star facing the place where the wedding will take place.*"[1]

This is similar to the concept of *muhurta* or *mahurat* in India which means—"*An auspicious time for an enterprise to begin or for a ceremony to take place...*"[2] In India, the religious heads of Hindus known as *pundits* are consulted before starting the preparation for marriage and the pundits ascertain the right time and day for the marriage preparations to begin. In India also, there are certain stellar/planetary positions that are avoided during the preparation of marriage as these stellar/planetary positions are considered to be inauspicious.

In India it is believed that a marriage is not only between two individuals, but between two families. It is not enough that the two individuals getting married like each-other and are compatible, but the two families should also like each-other and be compatible. That is why the tradition of arranged marriage is still going strong in India even today.

In Turkmenistan also it is not that different. Both the bride's and groom's families are totally involved in the marriage ceremonies. One more common thing in both these countries is that the moment a child is born the parents start to set money aside for their child's marriage. In India it specially happens if the child is a girl, since here there is a tradition, especially a Hindu tradition, of paying dowry

1. Turkmen Wedding Rites, Popular Beliefs, and Wedding Songs, n.d., Turkmenhost.com, 7 February 2015, http://www.turkmenhost.com/documents/Journal2/wedding.html
2. Language Matters, n.d., Oxford Dictionaries, 9 February 2015, http://www.oxforddictionaries.com/definition/english/mahurat

(*dahez*) to the groom's family for accepting the girl as their son's bride. In Turkmenistan, there is a similar tradition, only the other way round, known as '*kalym/galyn*', which is a kind of 'bride price'[1] paid to the bride's family by the groom's family. Hence, in Turkmenistan, the parents start saving money for the boy's wedding as soon as he is born! The common thing in both of these traditions is that the amount of '*dahez*' as well as '*kalym/galyn*' depends upon the social and monetary status of the families.

Another similar wedding tradition in India and Turkmenistan is that the vehicle that is supposed to carry the bride and groom to their home after the wedding ceremonies are over is decorated. In India, it is mostly flowers that are used as decoration for the vehicle. In Turkmenistan the vehicle is decorated with brightly-coloured scarves and ropes. It may be because of the fact that scarves have a special role to play in Turkmen women's lives. They wear colourful scarves, especially at weddings. There is a difference between how a married Turkmen woman wears her scarf and how an unmarried Turkmen girl wears hers. From the way a woman ties her headgear, it becomes clear that she is married or not. During the wedding ceremony, there is a tradition in Turkmenistan where after completion of the wedding rites, the newly-wed bride changes her 'maiden' headgear to a married-woman's headgear and gives away her 'maiden' scarf to a girl who is unmarried so that she might also have a successful wedding and married life.

In India there are many ornaments and objects that a married woman wears depending upon the region or State she belongs to. For instance, almost all Hindu married women wear vermilion (crimson-coloured powder known in India as '*sindoor*') at the centre of their foreheads near the start of their hairline. In Bengali culture, along with the vermilion, married women wear scarlet-coloured bangles with white bangles made usually of ivory. In the Northern

1. Victoria Clement, Culture of Turkmenistan, n.d., Countries and Their Cultures, 16 February 2015, http://www.everyculture.com/To-Z/T-rkmenistan.htmlhttp://www.everyculture.com/To-Z/T-rkmenistan.html

States of India like Uttar Pradesh, Punjab, and so on and Southern States of India like Maharashtra, Tamil Nadu and so on, married women, along with vermilion wear a black beaded gold necklace known as the '*mangalsutra*', although the size and shape may vary. In the Indian State of Punjab, along with vermilion and 'Mangalsutra', newly-married women wear '*choora/chooda*' (a set of 21 bangles in crimson and ivory colours in both the hands), especially for the first year of their married lives.

One thing in Turkmenistan which is different from India is that the wedding expenses are shared by both groom's and the bride's families. Turkmen as well as Indian weddings are quite an elaborate affair and sometimes there are more than 200 to 300 guests!

Rituals and Traditions Related to Birth in India and Turkmenistan

In India as well as in Turkmenistan, the rituals and traditions related to birth of a child start from the time a child comes into the womb of its mother. Pregnancy is celebrated with grandeur in both the countries. Becoming pregnant and subsequently, a mother are considered to be of utmost importance for a married woman. Though the marriage traditions of giving money to the groom's family in India and bride's family in Turkmenistan are opposite to each-other, the desire for a male-child is the same. The reason for the strong desire for a male-child is also the same; the continuation of progeny/ bloodline and the belief that a girl-child is a 'guest' in her own family and a boy stays and continues his family name and looks after the parents in old age. He also brings a new member to his family, i.e. his wife who helps the mother in her old age. There are even lullabies that reflect the desire for a son. Following are two lines of a Turkmen lullaby (in English): "*We feared that he would be a girl, thank God, he is a little man.*"[1]

---

1. Carole Blackwell, Tradition and Society in Turkmenistan: Gender, Oral Culture and Songs, (Great Britain: Routledge Publications, 2001) 29.

In her book "*Tradition and Society in Turkmenistan: Gender, Oral Culture and Song*" Carole Blackwell writes—"*The different reactions to the births of sons and daughters are often reflected in the names that parents choose.* ***Tagan****, the Turkmen word for 'tripod', is a name given to the third boy in a family. Just as the three legs of a tripod come together to bear a heavy weight, three sons will support their family. A fourth son is generally named* ***Chary****, a fifth* ***Baeshim****, and a sixth* ***Altyn****. There are no corresponding names for the third, fourth, fifth and sixth daughters. On the contrary, families with several girls often name one of them* ***Doyduk****, meaning 'we have enough'*."[1]

Naming of a newborn plays a vital role in India as well as Turkmenistan and hence there are elaborate naming ceremonies in these two countries. In India this naming ceremony is known as *Namkaran* ceremony. People of both these countries believe that a newborn should be named within 30-40 days of its birth, otherwise a long and strong existence of a child is not possible! In Turkmenistan there is a belief that the soul and name of a person are inseparable and hence one should not wait too long to name a newborn baby. There is also a belief that a newborn without a name will not survive long.

Before naming a baby in Turkmenistan, a *mullah* (a person belonging to the religious clergy) or a highly respected elderly man of the society is consulted. He reads out a prayer in the newborn's ears and then the newborn is named. Similarly, in India, the Hindus consult their religious clergy like a *pundit* and let him find out the first syllable of a newborn's name. The newborn is then named as per that first syllable. Sometimes, a baby might have two different names—one that is known to all and one known to only very close people and this 'secret name' is used only during religious ceremonies because more often than not, this 'secret name' is the name that is kept as per the syllable suggested by the *pundit* during the naming ceremony. The same tradition is there in Turkmenistan as well of using 'secret names' only for religious ceremonies. Turkmen people

1. Carole Blackwell, Tradition and Society in Turkmenistan: Gender, Oral Culture and Songs, (Great Britain: Routledge Publications, 2001) 62.

believe that a name should be chosen wisely as it affects the lifespan, character and well-being of a person.

Since infant mortality rate is quite high in Turkmenistan as well as in India, lot of care is taken to keep newborns safe and to ward off evil spirits or eyes that may befall on them. In Turkmenistan, amulets made of bones, shells, metals, especially silver etc. woven with a piece of cloth are hung on the crib or bed of a newborn or put on the newborn to protect it from evil. "***Aladja**, an amulet to protect from the evil eye, can be seen in all kinds of Turkmen arts and crafts. It is a lace made of knitted or woven and intertwined white and black threads. Thin aladja is worn on wrists, necks or sewn on dresses.*"[1] In India also there is a similar tradition. People attach amulets known as *tabeej/taweez* onto a newborn's arm or waist or neck to protect it from evil eyes.

Another important tradition in both India and Turkmenistan is the period of confinement for the mother and the newborn baby immediately after the birth of a child. This confinement period is supposed to be a recuperating period for the woman who just gave birth, so that she can have healthy pregnancies in the future as well, and for the new born this period is for adjusting to the world. "*The tradition arose from the need to protect both mum and baby from infection and help the mother recover from the exhaustion of childbirth*".[2]

The time period of the confinement is not important. What is important is the purpose behind it. During this confinement a mother is supposed to do minimum household work and rest as much as possible and the relatives, especially mother of the new mother or her mother-in-law takes care of the new mother as well as her newborn. During this confinement period it is made sure that the new mother

1. Adjap Bairieva, "Guard Me, My Talisman: Protective and Magic Elements in Turkmen Arts and Crafts", Turkmenistan International Magazine, 2006 N2-3: 11-12, Turkmenistaninfo.ru, 15 February 2015 http://www.turkmenistaninfo.ru/?page_id=6&type=article&elem_id=page_6/magazine_26/207&lang_id=en
2. "Post Delivery Confinement Practices in India", n.d., Babycenter, 15 February 2015, http://www.babycenter.in/a1021145/post-delivery-confinement-practices-in-india

eats the right kind of food so that her milk supply increases which in turn would keep the newborn healthy. In India, sometimes a *maalishwaali* (masseuse) is employed to massage the new mother during her confinement days to tighten her thigh muscles and to flatten her abdomen. The new mother in turn gives regular massages to her newborn so that his/her limbs grow stronger.

There is also an old tradition among women in India and Turkmenistan, which is that of tying a tight piece of cloth or belt around the abdomen to bring it back to the original size after the childbirth. "*A 59-year old woman in Garrygala spoke dismissively of young women today. She said that earlier generations of women recovered more quickly from pregnancy and childbirth because they observed all the old traditions and rituals...Her stomach soon returned to its original size, she said, because she bound it tightly with a leather strip with bells.*"[1] (Blackwell)

There are innumerable more rituals and traditions related to the birth of a child and its naming ceremony. A few have been selected to be mentioned here.

Rituals and Traditions Related to Death in India and Turkmenistan

Death is the ultimate truth of life. Death can be seen as a journey; as the culmination or the end, but also as a new beginning. Many cultures including the Indian and Turkmen believe that the spirit does return; that the physical end of a person does not mean his/her spiritual end. The spirit lives on; it is indestructible.

One of the common traditions of death ceremony is singing of lamentations by the women of the society. These lamentations are known as *agylar* in Turkmenistan and in India there are different names for such lamentations; one popular one is *rudaali*. There is also a tradition of hiring professional mourners at a funeral in many

1. Carole Blackwell, Tradition and Society in Turkmenistan: Gender, Oral Culture and Songs, (Great Britain: Routledge Publications, 2001) 60.

countries including India. The tradition of hiring professional mourners is an ancient one. There were professional mourners at pharaoh's funerals in ancient Egypt!

Since Turkmenistan is religion-wise and population-wise a Muslim dominated country, the burial rituals are as per the Islamic law. But one thing which is common in these rituals in India and Turkmenistan is that women are not allowed to participate in them, in the sense that they are not allowed to attend the actual funeral. In India, the male relatives and friends are allowed to accompany a deceased to the cremation site and a son or a father or a brother or a husband is allowed to burn the pyre. A daughter can take over but only under extreme circumstances. In Turkmenistan also male relatives and friends accompany the dead body to the burial ground. Probably that is why the ritual of mourning over the dead body by singing lamentations was started for women in India as well as in Turkmenistan, so that the women can say 'goodbye' to their loved ones from home only! Also, in both these countries the dead body is carried head first on a makeshift stretcher.

Although women in both these countries do not participate in cremation ceremony of the dead body, they do attend the feast which is hosted in the name of the deceased on particular days that are identified long ago by their ancestors. In Turkmenistan, the feast is held on the 7th day, the 40th day and after one year of death. "*Women do not attend funerals, but do participate in the commemoratory feasts held at seven days, forty days, and one year after a death.*"[1] In India, the feast is usually on the 12th day or the 13th day, the 40th day and also after one year depending upon the community, caste and religion. "*There are a certain number of days, depending on the community, after which the family is re-integrated into the society. That can happen after 13 days or 40 days – the specific number of days corresponds with caste*

1. Victoria Clement, Culture of Turkmenistan, n.d., Countries and Their Cultures, 16 February 2015, http://www.everyculture.com/To-Z/T-rkmenistan.htmlhttp://www.everyculture.com/To-Z/T-rkmenistan.html

and community."[1] Another article about death rites in India states the following – "*First Memorial – on the 3rd, 5th, 7th or 9th day, relatives gather for a meal of the deceased's favorite foods... On the 31st day, a memorial service is held... One-Year Memorial... At the yearly anniversary of the death... a priest conducts the shraddha (Death Rituals) rites in the home...*"[2]

Conclusion

Celebrations never end as long as an individual does not die! There are so many traditions and rituals and rites in each and every ceremony of a human life that it is near impossible to cover them all in just one article. Hence, it is unjust to claim that all the traditions and rituals are covered here. But, it was a serious endeavour to cover as many of the rituals and traditions of birth, marriage and death here as could be found out which are followed in India and Turkmenistan and to give a glimpse of the rituals and traditions that these two countries have in common. These rituals and traditions indicate that though people belong to different religions, different regions and countries, there is one thing common in them - that all of them are humans and human feelings transcend all borders.

References

Bhalla, Prem. Hindu Rites, Rituals, Customs and Traditions. New Delhi: Pustak Mahal, 2006.

Blackwell, Carole. Tradition and Society in Turkmenistan: Gender, Oral Culture and Song. Great Britain: Routledge Publications, 2001.

1. Dr. Vasudha Narayanan, Hindu Rituals for Death and Grief, n.d., Beliefnet, 18 February 2015, http://www.beliefnet.com/Faiths/Hinduism/2003/02/Hindu-Rituals-For-Death-And-Grief.aspx?p=1
2. Hindu Death Rituals and Beliefs, n.d., Mailerindia, 18 February 2015, http://www.mailerindia.com/hindu/veda/index.php?death

Khamsas of Nizami Ganjavi and Amir Khusrau

A Comparative Study

Sharif Husain Qasemi

Khamsa (Quintet) of Nizami of Ganja, now in Azarbaijan and that of Amir Khusrau-i- Dehlavi have been a subject of comparative study for long among the poets and critics of eminence. An attempt in brief is also being undertaken here in this respect.

Nizami Ganjavi (d. 599 A.H.) for the first time in the history of Persian poetry composed a *Khamsa*, and five *mathnavi's* in different meters and on different topics. [He has acknowledged that *Shahnama* of Firdausi and the works of Sanai have served as his models in composing *Khamsa*]. Thus Nizami actually created history in the annals of Persian poetry. It was such a tremendously artistic creation that in spite of a number of great and skillfully talented poets like Sa'di, Kamaluddin Isma'il, Humam Tabrizi and Auhadi Maraghi who enriched Persian poetry during hundred and fifty years or so just after Nizami, *Khamsa* remained unchallenged.

Then it was Amir Khusrau-i- Dehlavi (d. 725 / 1325) the greatest Persian poet of India by all standards, who dared to embark upon successfully composing a *Khamsa* after Nizami. This initiative of

Khamsa opened the doors for other poets in the Persian world and in India to compose *Khamsa*. Thus a good number of *Khamsas* came into being.

Nizami composed the following five *mathnavis* for his *Khamsa*:

1. *Makhzan-e-Asrar*, (treasury of mysteries) a dedicative poem, is the shortest and earliest of *Khamsa*.
2. *Khusrau Shirin* deals with the adventures of the Sessanian King Khusraw-Parvez and especially his love for the beautiful Shirin and the fate of his unhappy rival Farhad.
3. *Laila Majnun*, an Arab story, is one of the most popular works since Nizami's time.
4. *Haft Paikar*, seven portraits, is a legendary history of one of the Sassanian Kings namely Behram Gur.
5. *Iskandar Nama*, Alexander's book, is divided into two parts. The first one is named *Iqbal Nama*, book of Alexander's fortune. Second one is called *Khirad Nama*. Book of Alexander's wisdom.

These two parts are also named as *Sikandar Nama-i-Barri* and *Sikandar Nama-i-Bahri*.

Amir Khusrau's *Khamsa* includes the following five *mathnavis*:

1. *Matia'ui Anwar*, in repliy to Nizami's *Makhzan-e-Astar*. It practically deals with the same theme. Khusrau himself has summed up that he would discuss three things in this poem, the law the path and the truth. It was composed within only two weeks of time.

2. *Shirin-o-Khusrau* is the second *mathnavi* of Khusrau's *Khamsa*. The title of Nizami's *mathnavi* is *Khusrau Shirin*. Khusrau has reversed it to Shirin Khusrau. By doing so, he most probably, has given preference to the female character of the story. The story is almost the same as versified by Nizami. However, Khusrau-i-Dehlavi relates the old romance in a highly artistic style. The most authentic and sought after author on Khusrau Dr. Wahid Mirza sums up that,

Khusrau proves in this *mathnavi* to be a greater dramatist and more skilful painter of character than the old master. Similarly, the concluding part, where Khusrau questions the great philosopher, Buzurg Ummid about the skies, the stars, the four elements etc. is very original and instructive.

3. *Majnun-o-Laila*: Khusrau has also changed the title of this *mathnavi* from *Laila-o- Majnun* of Nizami to *Majnun-o-Laila* and informs that:

> *I have advanced close in his footsteps as far as I could. I discarded my own style and adopted his. I wrote after the old model and did away with all affectation, ornamenting my ideas with only simplicity and flow of language.*

Khusrau further claims that no one could imitate Nizami better than this.

> *If he (Nizami) himself had read my poem, he would not have recognized it from his own, and I see no difference between them except that one is the product of his mind and the other of my soul.*

There are however some variation in the details of the story of *Laila-o-Majnun* as narrated by these two master poets.

Nizami refers to the marriage of Ibn-e-Salam and Laila. Khusrau omits it in his version.

Similarly, Nizami makes no mention of Majnun's marriage to Naufal's daughter. Khusrau includes it in his *mathnavi*. Nizami, moreover introduces another romance in his version, i.e. the love and marriage of Zainab and Zaid which has been ignored by Khusrau.

Majnun-o-Laila is regarded as the finest poem of Khusrau's *Khamsa*. It is composed in an elegantly simple and tender style and for Khusrau this love had nothing of worldly desire about it, as it was a mystery from the treasure house of soul.

4. *A'ina-i-Sikandari*: Events narrated by Nizami and Khusrau in their *mathnavis* are almost the same. Khusrau, however, differs with Nizami in respect of the assertion of Nizami that Sikandar was a Prophet. Khusrau, on the other hand believes that Sikandar was only a saintly person. Similarly, Khusrau's *A'ina-i-Sikandari* also differs considerably from Nizami in several details. Khusrau has altogether left out the conquest of Persia and the death of Darius for, perhaps, it was difficult to tell those events better than Nizami had done. Allama Shibli No'mani calls *A'ina-i- Sikandari* a *dul* poem. Those who have gone through these two works of Nizami and Khusrau conclude that Khusrau has been less successful here than elsewhere in rising up to the level of the great master. Khusrau's heroic passages lack that vigour which Nizami's has so abundantly.

5. *Hasht Bahisht* (the Eight Paradises): It is the best poem of Khusrau's *Khamsa* composed in imitation of Nizami's *Haft Paikar*. It narrates the romantic life of Bahram Gur, the ancient Persian King known for his hunting expeditions. Khusrau says about his mathnavi that: *This poem is an echo of that old work and contains all the wealth which the old treasure has got. Honey, no doubt, is valuable but vinegar also has its purchasers, the pearl is costly, yet amber also possesses some value. And even if there be no real gold in this poem, it has the glitter of gold. A flower seller likes the garden; a wood cutter prefers a lot of trees. The bird of the desert that eats stones considers stones more valuable than pearls.*

It is formed by the seven stories told by the seven princesses all of which are apparently original and entertaining.

This is the real position of the *Khamsas* of Nizami and Khusrau. Now, some other points which would be referred to about these two *Khamsas* which would again help to ascertain the positions of the two. Nizami produced his *Khamsa* in not less than twenty seven years. He did not leave any other work worth mentioning except this *Khamsa*.

Khusrau, on the other hand was enormously productive. All of his literary creations are about three times more than that of Nizami.

Nizami, as mentioned just now, took twenty seven years to compose *Khamsa*, but Khusrau hastened to complete it only within the course of a little more than two years (698-701 A.H.). The reason for this haste in composing the *Khamsa* by Khusrau cannot be ignored as given by Dr. Wahid Mirza.

Khusrau, perhaps, later on realized the comparative futility of his attempt and got tired of the monotonous *mathnavi* verse, and so he hurried through the task as soon as possible.

But most probably, Khusrau as a great poet and a literary critic realized the fact that Nizami's *Khamsa* is endowed with original concerts, quaint similes and metaphors, picturesque and melodious phrases and vigorous expressions. And it is difficult to successfully imitate them. And so he got rid of this job hastily. This submission by Khusrau also supports this view.

> *"With this alphabet, which may amuse children, I have written an imitation of the great master's work. If it is not sweet, there is music in it, if there is no life in it, there is a skeleton. From his birth place Ganja, he scattered out the five treasures and with those five, I want to match my own strength, so that the wise one may say to me: Bravo! Thou worthy pupil of Nizami."*

Khusrau has acclaimed the verse of Nizami is like a pearl in its purity and the whole world is full of the pearls scattered by him.

Khusrau also recognizes the light he received from Nizami to traverse the literary path.

There are some poets and scholars who have expressed themselves on this topic. One of them was Ubaid, a poet associated with the court of Mohammad Tughlaq.

Khusrau was seriously studied at the court of Herat. Mirza Bayasangar (d. 837 A.H.) son of Shah Rukh Mirza and brother of Olugh Begh Timuri was the ruler of Herat. He was a poet himself and had developed literary taste. He was very much interested in Khusrau's works. After ceaseless efforts, he succeeded in collecting

120,000 verses of Khusrau. But having subsequently discovered 2000 more from his *ghazals*, he concluded that it would be difficult for him to collect the complete works of Khusrau and so gave up the idea forever. Mirza Bayasangar preferred *Khamsa* of Khusrau over Nizami's. But his brother Olugh Begh did not agree with him.

There is no other way but to accept Khusrau's view that, though he has successfully imitated Nizami, yet preference is given to Nizami's creation.

Both in India and Iran among the numerous *Khamsas* composed by various poets the *Khamsa* of Khusrau is far better by all standards.

Region

Afghanistan 2014
Challenges and Prospects

B.K. Sharma

Afghanistan is at the cusp of its chequered history, which is characterized by cycles of violence, punctuated briefly by uneasy peace. After more than a decade of violence and uncertainties, the steadfast and proud Afghan people are looking optimistic about a new dawn of opportunities to rebuild Afghanistan and usher a phase of durable security and peace. However, Afghanistan is at critical crossroads of its strategic destiny. The fledgling state faces a myriad of challenges due to threat from *Taliban* while the country is mired in impoverishment and governance deficit. These challenges are compounded by the withdrawal of US and NATO[1] forces amid the factional undercurrents in the country. The state capacity to stymie *Taliban* upsurge demands a major revamping with the help of international community. At the same time the political transition in the country is marked by uncertainties and needs deft political handling. On the positive side, the new era offers Afghanistan unique opportunities to gain from its salient geo-strategic position as a strategic bridge and buffer in the regional development and security. Afghanistan's geographic centrality lends itself as a conduit for transportation of trade and energy resources between Central Asia,

1. NATO – North Atlantic Treaty Organization

West Asia and South Asia thus changing the geopolitical landscape of the entire region. Afghanistan can also emerge as a rallying point for the international community to join hands in fighting the scourge of terrorism. This article briefly discusses some of the major challenges that Afghans face today and highlights the prospects for peace building in the conflict torn country.

Transformation of a Weak State

The decades of fighting have left Afghanistan in a dire state; it ranks very low in all the indices of economic well-being, human resource development and governance.

Key Indicators are summarized as under:

Table 1

Economic Indicators	*HDI*[1]	*Corruption*[2]	*GDP*[3]	*GDP (PPP)*[4]	*Fragile State Index*[5]
No. of Countries	(187)	(175)	(192)	(190)	(172)
Afghanistan	169	175	107	94	07
Pakistan	146	127	44	24	10
Iran	75	144	32	18	44
Uzbekistan	116	168	75	66	48
Kyrgyzstan	125	150	146	138	58
Tajikistan	133	154	139	134	55
Turkmenistan	103	168	90	88	74

1. Based on UNDP Report, released in 2014, 2013 rankings. http://hdr.undp.org/en/content/table-1-human-development-index-and-its-components
2. Corruption Perceptions Index 2013, released by Transparency International in 2014, http://www.transparency.org/cpi2013/results
3. World Bank GDP ranking (2013 figures) released in 2014. http://databank.worldbank.org/data/download/GDP.pdf
4. World Bank GDP PPP ranking (2013 figures) released in 2014. http://databank.worldbank.org/data/download/GDP_PPP.pdf
5. Fragile State Index 2014 Index. http://ffp.statesindex.org/rankings-2014

The biggest challenge that the National Unity Government faces is the economic transformation of the country with help of foreign aid (97 Percent) and poppy driven (50 percent of domestic economy) to a domestically strong and sustainable economy. The Afghan government will have to modernize agriculture and encourage people to grow crops and develop agro-based industries. Education, health, infrastructure, employment, combating corruption and providing good governance will have to be the major thrust areas to lift millions of people from morass of poverty to dignified living standards.

Afghanistan is endowed with rich natural resources. A 2007 United States Geological Service survey appears to have discovered nearly USD[1] 1 trillion in mineral deposits in Afghanistan. The Afghan government, however, feels the value is around USD 3 trillion. As per the survey, Afghanistan may hold 60 million tons of copper, 2.2 billion tons of iron ore, 1.4 million tons of rare earth elements such as lanthanum, cerium and neodymium, and lodes of aluminum, gold, silver, zinc, mercury and lithium. The mineral resources are yet to be fully surveyed and harnessed. Further, Afghanistan lacks rail and roadways infrastructure to transport its mineral resources. Hydropower is the main source of energy in Afghanistan. Due to prolonged war, power grids in Afghanistan are badly damaged. Only a third of population has access to electricity. Afghanistan generates around 600 megawatts (MW) of electricity at present but as per Da Afghanistan Breshna Sherkat (DABS) estimates the country will need around 3,000 MW to meet its requirements by 2020. Afghanistan is reported to have oil reserves totaling 2.9 billion barrels and also produces natural gas. Afghanistan is one of the participants in Turkmenistan–Afghanistan–Pakistan–India (TAPI) gas pipeline.

Besides a viable security environment, the Government will have to create an investor—friendly climate to attract foreign investors for the mining and other resource sectors. Afghanistan needs sustained external aid, technical expertise and dedicated commitment from

1. USD – US Dollars

the international community along with efficient management of funds at home by the political and administrative establishment.

Combating Narcotics

According to the report of Special Inspector General for Afghanistan reconstruction, released on 14 Oct 2014, there has been a 50 percent increase in poppy-related proceeds from 2012 to 2013 despite the US spending $7 billion for poppy eradication. Even Provinces that were once declared poppy free have seen resurgence in cultivation. Ironically, the production has increased due to use of deep well technology in previously non–arable land. Drug trafficking has been a main source of income for Taliban, warlords and corrupt-government officials. Drug addiction in Afghan society runs into generations since opium is taken as a medicine for alleviation of pain due to lack of medical facilities. Drug addiction, therefore, has had a phenomenal humanitarian security cost not only for Afghan society but international community at large. Central Asia has emerged as a major drug trafficking conduit to Russia and Europe. Narco-terrorism is a serious transnational threat that needs to be addressed collectively by all stakeholders.

Democratic Transition

Recent elections in Afghanistan have vindicated the people's faith in democracy vis-a-vis radical ideology professed by *Taliban*. The Presidential elections were peaceful, all ethnic groups participated enthusiastically and the election campaign was inclusive in nature. A record of over 50 percent voters cast their ballot, but the voting for the two leading candidates was on ethnic lines, each scoring more that 80 votes from their respective ethnic strongholds. The leadership has, however, shown remarkable maturity in circumventing the rigging crisis and bridging ethnic faultiness by inventing a new model of power sharing. The impending Loya Jirga is likely to endorse this transition from a strong presidency to a representative and participative framework, wherein the Prime Minister will play a significant role in running the government. However, this paradigm shift in run up to parliamentary elections in 2015 demands a careful handling of vexed nature of ethno-regionalism that dominates the Afghan politics. If this experiment of ethnic reconciliation fails the country runs the risk of plunging into serious ethnic strife much to the benefit of despotic *Taliban*. The Afghan Government will have to work overtime to create a desired equilibrium in the power sharing arrangement albeit with substantial outside help from democratic countries to build its institutions and create mechanisms that are necessary to broaden and deepen the roots of democracy in the country. Most import task is to strengthen the national character of Afghan National Security Forces (ANSF) and ensure that its rank structure and cadres do not drift on ethnic lines.

Security Environment

Taliban and *Al Qaeda* continue to pose a formidable threat not only to Afghanistan but also to the entire neighborhood. These forces are adherents of a militant *Salfi-Wahabi* ideology that seeks creation of a Caliphate, i.e. establishing *Nizam-e-Mustafa* (Sharia Law). They are opposed to the concept of Westphalian democratic states and reject the concept of sovereignty of the people. They seek to expand their influence in the entire region by creating the mythical state of Khurasan, encompassing the territory of Caucasus, Central Asia, Xinjiang Province, Afghanistan-Pakistan region, Indian sub-continent etc. Outwardly, there are a number of Islamist radical groups that appear disparate and divergent in their objectives. *Haqqani* network and *Hiz-e-Islami* are active in Afghanistan. *Tehrik-e-Taliban* of Pakistan (TTP) and *Jundullah* are fighting the Pakistan Government whereas, groups like *Lashkar-e-Taiba*, *Hizul Mujahideen* and *Jaishe Mohamed* are protégé of ISI, directed against India. Likewise, groups like Islamic Movement of Uzbekistan, Uzbek Islamic Jihad, Hizb-e-Tehrir, Jund-al-Khalifa are active in Central Asia and have linkages with Jaish-al-Muhajireenwal Ansar active in Caucasus and East

Turkistan Islamic Movement operating in the Xinjiang province. The rise of Islamic State of Iraq and *Al Sham* (ISIS) has added a new dimension to the idea of universal *Jihadi* movement drawing cadres from the western countries. *Al Qaeda* is striving hard to retain its leadership in the Pan–Islamist movement by upping the ante. Declaration of formation of *Al Qaeda* in Indian sub-continent is a move in this direction. Meanwhile, the extreme brand of *Jihad* demonstrated by the ISIS has created its appeal in Pakistan, Kashmir and Afghanistan. There are reports of fair number of *Jihadi* cadres from this region training with the ISIS. Some splinter groups of the TTP have already owed allegiance to the ISIS and would be tempted to emulate ISIS brand of Jihad in the Afghanistan-Pakistan region. The experts believe that array of *Jihadi* outfits may pursue different tactical objectives but they are united in their overall ideological goal of creating a Caliphate. Therefore, their Pan Islamist outlook propels them to forge alliances in favour of their larger religious cause. Such a propensity in these forces needs to be contested.

The failure of ANSF and Pakistan's Establishment to contain resurgent Taliban and other *Jihadi* outfits will have serious consequences for the Afghanistan-Pakistan region with wider ramifications for Central Asia and Xinjiang province. Particularly susceptible to *Jihadi* influence is Fergana valley in Central Asia where the traditionally orthodox population faces a perceived sense of relative deprivation and ethnic divide. Complicated succession of unstable regimes in Central Asia can inadvertently provide a spark to ignite the situation thus setting the stage for Jihadist to fish in troubled waters. De-stabilization of Afghanistan–Pakistan region, Central Asia and Xinjiang province will have unintended consequences for China's Silk Route dream project, flow of energy resources from the Caspian region and operationalization of Pakistan Economic corridor. Likewise, emboldened Jihadists have potential to escalate violence in Kashmir, push India-Pakistan towards a military confrontation and scuttle the prospects of Turkmenistan-Afghanistan-Pakistan–India (TAPI) pipeline. It is therefore pertinent that the regional countries are cognizant of this larger transnational threat that can destabilize the region. Therefore defeat of *Taliban* in Afghanistan-Pakistan region is a 'sine quo non' for regional security. More pertinent in this regard is the role of Pakistan, which has thus far, used these non-state actors as instruments of state policy to pursue its flawed security agenda against India and Afghanistan. It is high time Pakistan realizes that chickens have come home to roost. Today, the Government of Pakistan considers *Jihadi* violence a principal threat to its national security and has embarked upon a counter insurgency campaign named *Zarb-e-Azb* in Waziristan albeit with a limited success. However, its policy of supporting *Haqqani* network and anti-India militant groups has not tangibly changed. It is time that Pakistan changes its mindset and sheds duplicity in dealing with different militant outfits differently.

Prospects of Peace Building in Afghanistan

Fighting Terrorism

Post 2014, the US will have approximately 9500 plus 2000 troops deployed in combat support role in Afghanistan under the rubric of recently signed Bilateral Security Agreement and the State of Forces Agreement. The reduction of foreign troops will saddle the ANSF with an onerous responsibility of defending the nation against heavy odds. ANSF has given an excellent account of its capability and indomitable spirit to fulfill its role as seen during the election period by not succumbing to the *Taliban*. The shortage of arms and ammunition often hampers the forces from giving an even more befitting response to anti national elements. To this end, the international community, particularly the US, has a moral obligation to render maximum support to ANSF in terms of intelligence, artillery/air support, logistics and training. The future role of International Security Assistance Force (ISAF) is crucial and necessary to pursue its unfinished mandate in Afghanistan and protect its image in the eyes of Afghan people for the promises made to them. It would be prudent for the US to reconsider its unilateral decision to withdraw from Afghanistan precipitously and fulfill its security obligations in conformity with security situation on ground.

It is imperative for India, Afghanistan and its neighbors, US/ NATO and Russia to join hands in fight against terrorism. These countries, except Turkmenistan, are members of or observers in the Shanghai Cooperation Organization (SCO). Likewise, Russia and three Central Asian states (Kazakhstan, Tajikistan, Kyrgyzstan) are members of the Collective Security Organizations (CSTO). Both these organizations have established Anti Terrorists Centres in Central Asia and regularly conduct joint military training to combat terrorism. On the other hand, NATO under the Programme for Peace (PfP) is engaged in capacity building against non-traditional threats in the region. The regional leadership and these organizations should assiduously shed their traditional mindsets and explore the avenues for creating a collaborative security framework and mechanisms to foster cooperation between NATO, SCO and CSTO to fight terrorism.

Afghanistan the New Epicenter of Co-Prosperity

Peace building in Afghanistan should be Afghan inspired and Afghan driven with international community fulfilling its commitments of civil aid made during series of Donor Conferences held during last 14 years. There is a need for foreign countries to closely cooperate with the Afghan government on the type of assistance, financial, technology and expertise they need and leave it to the Afghan government for its actual implementation. The focus should be on the outcomes and not on the bureaucratic procedures. The assistance rendered should be based on the local aspirations and not decided arbitrarily by outsiders. In the ultimate analysis, the best thing would be the creation of an enabling environment for early construction of new strategic transportation and energy grids from Central Asia/West Asia to South Asia via Afghanistan. The opening of Chabahar–Zaranj–Delaram road will connect Afghanistan with Iran and India and provide this land-locked country an alternate access to the Arabian

Sea. The route will also provide the largest regional economy India direct connection to Central Asia. Early operationalization of North-South corridor will further boost inter regional commerce and trade. The Turkmenistan-Afghanistan-Pakistan-India (TAPI) and Iran-Pakistan-India (IPI) gas pipelines: popularly called the '*pipelines of peace*' will boost energy cooperation between energy–rich Central Asia and energy—starved South Asia. The return of peace will also facilitate completion of electricity grid under CASA-1000 programme that envisages export of electricity from Tajikistan/Kyrgyzstan to Pakistan via Afghanistan. The realization of these projects will go a long way in integrating regional economies, earn huge transit fees for Afghanistan, generate employment opportunities for youth of Afghanistan and promote peace between India and Pakistan.

Role of India

India has made significant contribution in peace building in Afghanistan by assisting the ANSF in capacity building and constructing civil infrastructure. India has spent about $2 billion on various projects in Afghanistan. India is committed to support the new Afghanistan Government under the aegis of strategic partnership agreement signed between the two countries. India is against any Zero-Sum outlook on Afghanistan and favours an inclusive and collaborative approach to peace building in the country. The signs of rapprochement between President Ghani and Pakistan establishment are being watched with keen interest. China's commitment to aid reconstruction of Afghanistan, promote trade and humanitarian assistance is also appreciated. As far as Pakistan–Afghanistan relations are concerned, while there is scope for improving economic and trade ties, enhancing regional connectivity, rehabilitating refugees, the Pakistan military must also show greater willingness to crack down on *Taliban* sanctuaries on its side of the border. Its recent offensive against TTP hideouts in North Waziristan is welcomed, but it must broaden the crackdown to include all terrorist groups that operate in the region. The TTP has links to terrorist groups that attack

Afghanistan (and India), as well as *Al Qaeda*, and exploits Pakistan's permissive policies toward other terrorist groups to conduct its own anti-government attacks. Thus, maintaining a selective approach to targeting terrorists not only jeopardizes Pakistan's efforts to improve regional relationships, it puts the country's internal security at risk and leads to attacks like the one that occurred at Wagah. It is hoped to see a better cooperation between Pakistan and Afghanistan in effective monitoring of terrorist movement across the Durand line and coordination in destroying terrorist strongholds on both sides of the border. However, it is strongly advocated to expand these bilateral initiatives to a comprehensive multi–lateral level wherein all stakeholders fulfill their obligations for security and development of Afghanistan. The international community and major donors of Afghanistan should tie their aid and economic assistance programmes to key reforms in the public institutions—such as fighting corruption, reforming of the judiciary, implementing the rule of law, improving sub-national governance, and improving Afghanistan's public finance management system. Condition-based provision of aid pushes for much needed hard reforms in Afghanistan while also giving President Ghani and his team the justification needed to satisfy the Afghan public that in the absence of these reforms Afghanistan will have difficult time securing foreign aid.

Role of Turkmenistan

President of Afghanistan, Mr. Ashraf Ghani, at the time of taking over reins of power made a laudatory statement alluding to future of Afghanistan, "*history will not be repeated, we have overcome the past*". In its quest for a promising future of Afghanistan, Turkmenistan has played and will continue to play a significant role in the peace and security of that country. Turkmenistan's principle-based foreign policy of Neutrality makes it as one the most acceptable interlocutor or facilitator in engaging with divergent players in Afghanistan. It has done a great deal to improve connectivity in the border districts of Afghanistan besides supplying of electricity and constructive initiatives. In fact the Centre for Preventive Diplomacy established at Ashgabat by the UN can play a stellar role in the resolution of conflict and building peace not only in Afghanistan but in the entire region. Turkmenistan enjoys the good will of the people and contending parties in Afghanistan and is well poised to contribute in the process of peace and development in the region. It being the fountainhead of TAPI can dramatically improve the economic landscape of the region and usher peace and tranquility.

Contributors

Afzal, Mohammed, *Former Member of Parliament, Ambassador of India to Turkmenistan, Patron*: Indo-Turkman Friendship Society of India.

Agnihotri, Mona, *PhD Scholar*, Centre of Russian Studies, School of Language, Literature and Culture Studies, Jawaharlal Nehru University, New Delhi. *Guest Faculty*, Delhi University. *Member of Indian History Congress*, Published Author of Semi-autobiographical English Novel.

Anil, R.N., *Founder and Secretary General* of Unity International Foundation and Friends of Central Asia Forum.

Burynow, A.A., *The Head of Social Sciences Department of Magtymguly*, Turkmen State University, Candidate of Philosophy, Associate Professor.

Deshpande, Sanjay, *Director*, Centre for Central Eurasian Studies, University of Mumbai.

Godarov, Rahmanberdi, *Deputy-Director on Science*, National Institute of Manuscripts, The Academy of Sciences, Turkmenistan.

Joshi, Nirmala, *Former Professor at the Jawaharlal Nehru University*, New Delhi, *Director*, India Central Asia Foundation, New Delhi. *Research Advisor*, United Service Institution of India, New Delhi.

Kuleyev, Durdymyrat, Turkmen State Institute of Culture, Turkmenistan.

Kundu, Nivedita Das, Ph.D in International Studies and Eurasia Expert. *Senior Research Advisor*, United Service Institution of India, New Delhi, India.

Mittal, Manu, *Professor*, Centre of Russian Studies, School of Language, Literature and Culture Studies, Jawaharlal Nehru University, New Delhi, India. *Convener*, Silk Road Studies Programme JNU, Jawaharlal Nehru University, New Delhi, India.

Narain, Meeta, *Professor*, Centre of Russian Studies, SLL&CS, Jawaharlal Nehru University, New Delhi, India.

Qasemi, Sharif Husain, *Professor*, University of Delhi, Delhi, India.

Rahmanov, Amangeldi, *Head*, Department of International Relations and Diplomacy, Institute of International Relations, Ministry of Foreign Affairs of Turkmenistan. Ambassador Extraordinary and Plenipotentiary.

Shah, Naseem Ahmad, *Director*, Institute of Islamic Studies, Kashmir University, Kashmir, India. Research Paper Contributor focusing on the commonalties and similarities in the writings of the poets - Noor Mohammad Andaleeb, Dawlat Muhammad Azadi and Magtymguly Pyragy and their Indian counterparts. Recipient of Magtymguly Award in recognition of his contribution in highlighting the Turkmen literary legacy by way of translating into Urdu language the prominent poems of Turkmen national poet Magtymguly Pyragy.

Sharma, B.K., *Major General, Head* Centre for Strategic Studies and Simulation, United Service Institution of India, New Delhi, India.

Wasey, Akhtarul, *Professor*, Commissioner for Linguistic Minorities in India (A Constitutional Authority under Article 350 B of the Constitution of India). *Formerly, Head*, Department of Islamic Studies. *Director*, Zakir Husain Institute of Islamic Studies, Jamia Millia Islamia, New Delhi, India.

Index

Index